Converts and Kingdoms

Diane Moczar

Converts and Kingdoms

*How the Church Converted the Pagan West—
and How We Can Do It Again*

CATHOLIC
ANSWERS
PRESS

SAN DIEGO
2012

Published by Catholic Answers, Inc.
2020 Gillespie Way
El Cajon, California 92020
888-291-8000 orders
619-387-0042 fax
www.catholic.com

Typesetting by Nora Malone
Cover design by Devin Schadt
Map Illustrations by Tim Evans

Printed in the United States of America

ISBN 978-1-933919-57-7

I would like to acknowledge the invaluable help I received from my editor, Todd Aglialoro, in writing this book. It was his skill in pruning (however painful to the author ...), suggesting new approaches to knotty questions, and helping to polish the whole thing that made it into the interesting and instructive read that I hope it now is.

*To the memory of the late Dr. Warren Carroll,
whose many works on the history of Christendom,
the Russian Revolution, and other important
historical topics have fascinated and instructed
a whole generation of Catholic readers.*

Contents

Foreword by Rev. C. John McCloskey 9

Introduction. 13

1. Constantine and the Conversion of Rome 19

2. The Eldest Daughter of the Church 47

3. The Sceptered Isle and the Emerald Isle 79

4. Barbarians of the Borderlands 103

5. The Ancient Faith in a New World. 131

6. Rebellion and Reconversion 157

Conclusion 181

Bibliography 185

Foreword

Okay, I confess. My two favorite Church historians of this century and the last are the late Warren Carroll and Diane Moczar, the author of this book. Why? Simply because Carroll was and Moczar is a fully credentialed historian who clearly believes that the Catholic Church is the Body of Christ and who makes the history of the Church excitingly page-turning while not being fictional. They write from a faith perspective that recognizes the strengths and weaknesses of the members of the Church, from popes to laymen, who populate their pages, but they recognize that all will be well in the end. After all, we await the *Parousia*, which we all will experience either in this life or in the life above (we hope!).

This most recent volume by Professor Moczar deals with great conversions to Catholicism through the centuries and down to our own time, conversions that have had an outsized impact not only on the Church but also on the world we live in.

Some of the individual converts were kings who brought all their subjects along for the ride to salvation. Others, like St. Patrick and St. Juan Diego, experienced mystical encounters or inspirations, revelations, or apparitions that changed their lives and won whole nations and even continents to Catholicism.

Or think of St. Ignatius, founder of the Society of Jesus, who converted from a life of sin when he was deprived of the pulp fiction of his era and in desperation picked up some classics of spiritual reading while convalescing from battle wounds. Through his resolute "yes" to Christ the whole Orient was eventually opened to the work of the Holy Spirit.

Of course there are various roads to conversion. Most readers have probably experienced the most common one without any memory of it. This is the sacrament of baptism administered in infancy, thanks to loving parents and to the loving desire of God the Father to adopt newborn children as his own sons and daughters. From the time of the apostles, however, there has been another and often more dramatic experience of conversion, that of previously unbaptized adults. There are, for example, the spectacular conversions of the first centuries of Christianity and the gradual en masse conversion of the barbarian tribes and nations over the course of almost 900 years—among whom the ancestors of most of the readers of this book are included. These conversions produced what we call the West or Christendom.

Thanks to the heroic missionaries and to ongoing globalization, the Church continues to grow and win converts in Africa and the Far East. Yet the West, cradle of the faith, is in serious peril due to scientism, consumerism, practical atheism, mass apostasy, and other ills. Who knows? Perhaps Africa and the Far East will re-evangelize us to return the favor. We have the assurance that the Church will always be here until the Lord comes to judge the living and the dead, but that could be any time from tomorrow to a billion years hence.

The Church started with twelve apostles, and in a little more than 2,000 years it has never had a down year; it is always growing, producing new saints and laying new foundations to face the challenges of the age. In his book *The Nature and Mission of Theology,* Pope Benedict XVI tells us: "This is why in every age the path to faith can take its bearings by converts; it explains why they in particular can help us to recognize the reason for the hope that is in us (1 Pet. 3:15) and to bear witness to it. The connection between faith and theology is not therefore some sort of sentimental or pietistic twaddle but is a direct consequence of the logic of the thing and is corroborated by the whole of history."

Diane Moczar has written a marvelous book about great converts—many of them saints, others not—who changed not just the Church but also the destiny of human civilization. But remember, we live in the present, not the past. In recent years, as many as a million Americans have converted to Catholicism. How did this happen?

It happened in many different ways, tailored to the needs, desires, strengths, and weaknesses of each soul. However, almost all converts testify to having one thing in common: the example of a friend, relative, or co-worker who at some point in their journey asked them, "Have you ever thought of becoming a Catholic?"

Now, how many times have you asked that question of others? For when you do, when accompanied by prayer and sacrifice and true friendship, you may find *yourself* an instrument of the Holy Spirit for the conversion of great Catholics who will change the world.

Rev. C. John McCloskey III is a Church historian and research fellow at the Faith and Reason Institute in Washington, D.C. His website is www. frmccloskey.com.

Introduction

It is hard to imagine living in a world without Christianity—not just a world without the Church but a world without a culture and civilization that were formed by the Church and permeated with Christian principles. The secular states of the West today operate, at least to some extent, according to ideas of social justice and human dignity that go back many centuries to the time when those states were Catholic.

How did they become Catholic in the first place? We are familiar with the conversion stories of individuals such as St. Augustine and Bl. John Henry Newman, but what of the conversion of entire nations? Beginning with the spread of the Church within the Roman Empire soon after the Resurrection and Ascension of Christ, the wave of conversion spread slowly outward until, by modern times, it had reached virtually "all nations." How did that unlikely thing happen, when all those nations were pagan in the first place?

This is the tale we are going to tell in this book: the tale of the creation of the civilization known as Christendom.

For each conversion story discussed in the following chapters, there are three groups to be considered:

The Converted

Who were the people, both the individuals—insofar as we know them—and the nations that entered the Church in the early ages of Christendom? What was their background and what attracted them to the faith? Their characters, cultural levels, and reasons for conversion varied greatly, as did the rapidity of their entrance into the Church. Some seem to have been won over almost instantly upon coming to the knowledge of Christianity, whereas for others it took much longer—a lifetime in the case of some individuals, and generations for some nations. What was the process by which worshippers of Mithra or Baal were led to renounce their false gods?

The Converters

Leaving aside the rare instances of persons who became Catholic because of some private revelation or heavenly visitation, conversions required converters: apostles who spread the knowledge of Christianity to those who did not know it. These may have been trained apologists whose mission it was to convert individuals and entire nations, a Catholic spouse married to an unbeliever, even a Christian slave girl who managed to interest her mistress in the Church. While all these zealous apostles had the same goal, the means they employed varied widely. In some cases, miracles abounded throughout the apostle's career; in other cases, he had to brave furious resistance on the part of pagan or even diabolical forces. Not a few of the messengers of the good news met with violent resistance that brought about their martyrdom.

From heaven, however, they continue their work even more effectively, as the Catholic history of a number of nations demonstrates. Whether those in organized religious orders, solitary hermits, scholars, or ordinary individuals burning to bring souls to Christ, the converters and their methods are well worth getting to know.

The Enemies

There is, of course, one primary Enemy behind the numerous antagonists who have sought from the time of Christ himself to obstruct and, if possible, destroy his Church. Throughout the centuries these antagonists have had a great variety of motives, in addition to their antipathy for Catholicism, that caused them to fight the spread of the Church. Some of those in the enemies category include:

- *Entrenched religious establishments.* The Gospels attest to the hostility of the Jewish priests and their associates, both to Christ and—after they managed to have him crucified—to the apostles and other Christians, including the first martyr, St. Stephen. Elsewhere in the Roman Empire there were powerful local pagan hierarchies. As the empire crumbled, there were also heretics such as the Arians, who had acquired a large following among the barbarians who were also fighting against the Church and its missionaries.

- *Sorcerers such as Simon Magus,* whose saga is described in the Acts of the Apostles (8, 9-24). The prevalence of witchcraft and sorcery in the ancient world isn't discussed much today, but the early Fathers of the Church refer frequently to the real power of the sorcerers and their ability to counterfeit miracles to discredit Christian preachers. We will see these sinister and formidable enemies turn up repeatedly in our conversion stories.

- *Political enemies.* In the ancient and medieval worlds, religious and political establishments often overlapped, and we will observe them frequently joining forces to prevent the conversion of those subject to them. Many of the Roman emperors who persecuted the Church do not seem to have been especially devoted to paganism, but they worked to stamp out the new religion—with the support of the Roman bureaucracy. They did this out of a conviction that Christianity somehow threatened Roman political institutions and the Roman way of life. Throughout the Roman world, local political authorities, whether sincerely attached to paganism or not, were often hostile to new ideas that might rock their governmental boats. Christians, who frequently freed their slaves and respected women as the equals of men, caused alarm everywhere. When rumors of their sinister religious practices were added to the tale, hostility often became persecution.

• *Economic interests.* The economic motive for antipathy to Christianity is often overlooked, but it sometimes played an important role in anti-Christian attitudes. We do not often consider how far the pagan religion affected Roman economic life, from the numerous idol-makers and idol-sellers whose livelihood depended on pagan practices to the large number of Romans of all classes associated with temple worship; builders, priests, priestesses, and providers of sacrificial victims were all affected by the collapse of paganism. (Pity those unemployed Vestal Virgins, too.)

• *Mobs.* In the large cities of the Roman Empire in particular, outbreaks of rioting and disorder were easily fomented and could often be deadly. Religious, political, and economic enemies of the Christians had little trouble stirring up crowds against them, with deadly effect. Popular hostility would dog Christian missionaries and communities throughout the empire, aroused by the sorcerers, heretics, and pagan authorities that Christianity sought to replace. That these riots were often unpredictable made them even more dangerous for the followers of Christ.

Given the number and variety of enemies arrayed against the Church from the beginning, its spectacular success in the course of the centuries is remarkable—nothing short, in fact, of miraculous. It is our theme in this work.

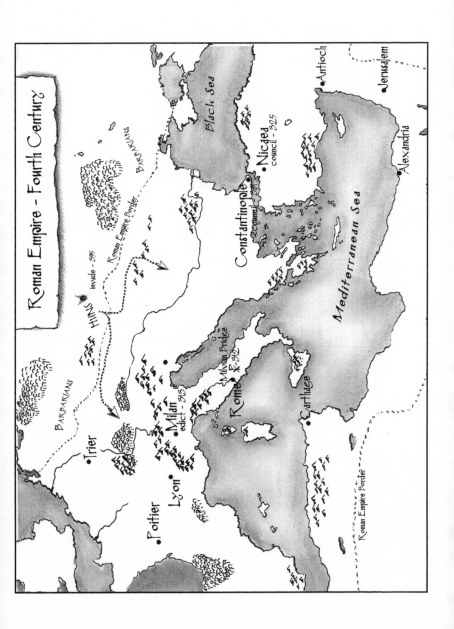

Roman Empire – Fourth Century

HUNS
invade - 395

BARBARIANS

Roman Empire Border

BARBARIANS

Black Sea

Trier

Poitier

Lyon

Milan
edict - 313

Rome
Milvian Bridge
R. 312

Constantinople
2 council - 381

Nicaed
council - 325

Carthage

Mediterranean Sea

Antioch

Jerusalem

Alexandria

Roman Empire Border

Constantine and the Conversion of Rome

The Roman Empire at its height sprawled across the map from Britain to Mesopotamia, along the North African coast, and northward into Germany and modern Hungary. The Mediterranean Sea was a Roman lake. This empire on the whole was firmly pagan. How likely was it, then, that a tiny group of Christians from the backwater of Palestine, ordered by their Founder to spread his teachings throughout the world, would actually be able to carry them within a few years to the heart of Rome itself? This seemingly impossible feat was accomplished, however, much of it within a few decades of the Pentecost and despite the persecutions that immediately followed the birth of the Church.

By the fourth century, Christianity had spread from Christ's birthplace in the Roman province of Palestine to most of the Roman Empire. One has only to read the Acts of the Apostles and the epistles of St. Paul to realize how seriously the early Christians took our Lord's command to bring the gospel to "all nations." Recent discoveries even suggest that the Church had reached as far as China by A.D. 86.[1]

Besides the work of the apostles, their helpers, and others who dedicated their lives to spreading the faith, there were legions of "amateur" missionaries throughout the empire. Some of them were slaves who traveled long distances with their masters and passed on the good news to other slaves (and sometimes their masters) whom they met on their journeys. Soldiers, transferred from one Roman territory to another, passed on what they had heard of Christ. (St. Martin of Tours, for example, the great apostle of Roman Gaul whom we will meet later on, was a Roman soldier.) Merchants, too, traveled long distances on business and

---

[1] The discoveries have been covered in the press in recent years. For photographs and a summary of the theory, see www.christianityinchina.org.

spread the news and the stories they heard. The famous roads that the Romans built every place they conquered made travel, and consequently the spread of all kinds of news—including the "good news"—relatively easy. Furthermore, the Mediterranean Sea made the coasts of Egypt, North Africa, and southern Europe accessible to Christians from Palestine.

There was, of course, a downside to being one of those who helped spread the faith: you might be slowly tortured to death for public entertainment. The first persecution of Christians in Rome began shortly after the organization of a small Catholic (the word is used from the first century) community in the capital of the empire. The emperor at the time was Nero, one of the notoriously unbalanced holders of that office, and his apparent motive was to shift the blame for a great fire in the city from himself to the Christians. (He does not, in fact, seem to have started the fire and was not even in the city when it began. He got the blame because of his passion for urban renewal, which had led him to have large parts of the city razed so that he could rebuild them in what seemed to him better style.) Hence the first Roman persecution, in A.D. 64, which continued off and on for years and during which both Peter and Paul were martyred.

Persecutions continued, sometimes sporadically, sometimes for long stretches, for the next three centuries. They could be local affairs—small groups denounced to a governor for refusing to offer sacrifice to the Roman gods—or empire-wide holocausts. None of this stopped the development and spread of the Church: missionaries still made converts; parents still passed on the faith to the children, though in great secrecy; theologians still codified doctrine and combated heresies that sprang up; Catholics still heard Mass in the catacombs or in the cellars of private homes. Christian soldiers fought in the Roman army and Christians worked for the Roman government, unless and until they were found out and ordered to give that pinch of incense to Jupiter.

In the late third century, things took a turn for the worse for Christians of the Roman Empire. With the reign of Emperor Decius in the 250s, legislation was issued ordering compliance with the religion of Rome on pain of death. This was the first empire-wide persecution, and it made many martyrs. Later emperors did not enforce those laws, so the Church had a semi-respite until Diocletian came on the scene at the end of the century. He was in some ways a great emperor, able to deal effectively with barbarian incursions as well as economic and agricultural problems. He also managed to stave off the dissolution of the shaky empire by dividing it so that there were two emperors (each with the title of Augustus), one in the east and one in the west, each assisted by a sort of sub-emperor with the title of Caesar.

Diocletian's fellow Augustus, unfortunately, was a man named Galerius whose mother had been a pagan priestess; mother and son both seem to have hated the Christians, and it may have been these two who egged Diocletian, himself no friend of Christianity, to launch the empire-wide persecution of 303 for which he is infamous. It was to be the worst of the persecutions thus far; it lasted for 10 years and was characterized by the most hideous tortures yet seen. In 304, Diocletian seems to have had a health crisis or possibly a nervous breakdown; he went into seclusion and abdicated the following year. Galerius kept the persecution going, but a few years later he was struck by a hideous illness that he seemed to interpret as a punishment from the Christian God, and shortly before his death in 311 he issued an edict of toleration for Christianity. In it, he actually asked the Christians to pray that their God would spare him and the empire. Unfortunately, his successor and nephew, Maximinus Daia, resumed the persecution in the areas under his control, in addition to launching a full-fledged propaganda campaign to destroy the credibility of the new religion of Christ.

Thus things continued until the "divine surprise" of the accession to the imperial throne of the son of a saint.

Constantine the Great

In the political chaos that followed the retirement of Diocletian and the illness of Galerius, a number of men vied for power, among them Constantius I, whom Galerius had chosen as Augustus in the west in 305. He does not seem to have been a Christian, though he was the Roman ruler who did the least to carry out the persecution ordered by Diocletian and Galerius. This may have been due to the influence of his first wife, St. Helena. He was also thought by some chroniclers of the period to have worshiped one god, either Apollo or the sun god, rather than the traditional assortment of pagan deities. If this was the case, it might explain his reluctance to persecute other monotheists.

We know almost nothing about the life of Constantius's wife, Helena, before the time of her son's accession to power; we do not even know whether she was born into a Christian family or became a convert at Constantine's court. She was said to have been of humble origin, possibly an innkeeper or servant whom Constantius met on his travels. Having given him a son, Constantine, she was later divorced by her husband so that he could make a more politically advantageous match, whereupon she left his court and went to live in the imperial city of Trier.

Constantine, meanwhile, was now a young man at the court of the Eastern emperor, Galerius, in Nicomedia. Already an experienced commander, he had expected to be made Caesar when his father became Augustus of the Western Empire, but was passed over. Hearing that his father was ill and had sent Galerius a letter asking that his son be allowed to come to him, Constantine did not wait for permission. He took off secretly on a rapid journey across Europe before any of his rivals could stop him, and met up with his father on the coast of Gaul, where he was preparing to cross over to Britain to fight the Picts. Father and son went together, and before Constantius died the following year he commended his son to the Roman army stationed in Britain.

The army enthusiastically, though irregularly, proclaimed Constantine Augustus in place of his father; Galerius agreed to a role for Constantine in the imperial hierarchy, but only as a Caesar. Constantine, however, preferred the army's vote and determined to enforce his claim to the imperial title. Thus began the often lurid political career of Helena's son, who would become ruler of the Western Empire and then sole emperor. More importantly, he would be a key figure in changing the Roman Empire from a pagan to a Christian realm.

There were many obstacles in the young commander's path to the heights of power, in particular his in-laws. Constantine was married to Fausta, the daughter of a former Augustus of the west named Maximian. Being an older man and former Augustus, Maximian may have resented playing second fiddle to his son-in-law in the Roman campaigns to secure imperial borders against the increasing numbers of invading barbarians. He could not make up his mind to leave the job to younger men, and kept retiring, regretting it, and coming back on the political scene to stir things up. Maximian was even said to have mounted a rebellion against Constantine and then plotted to assassinate him.

The most lurid tale has it that the plot was foiled when Fausta revealed it to her husband. Constantine had a slave sleep in his bed while he lay in wait for Maximian, who crept into the room and killed the slave, thinking it was Constantine. He came out holding his dripping dagger and crying, "Fausta, Fausta, the tyrant is dead!" Then, of course he saw—reading from left to right—Constantine and Fausta. He was put in prison, and most sources agree that he died there, though they differ as to whether he was murdered by Constantine or committed suicide. In any case, Maximian was out of the way, but his son Maxentius was not.

The Sign in the Sky

In the spring of 312, Constantine set out for Rome, where Maxentius had taken control by quelling an uprising and gaining the support of powerful factions. He was in much the same position as Constantine, having also been passed over for the office of Caesar by Galerius in favor of another man. Now that he was in control of Rome, he wavered between calling himself Caesar and Augustus; in any case, he was the obvious rival of Constantine for sole rule in the Western Empire, and he held Rome. He was also anxious to avenge the death of his father and unwilling to compromise with his murderer.

Constantine was ambitious, but he was also superstitious. A popular pagan cult, particularly favored by the military, was that of Mithra, a Zoroastrian deity with whom was associated, at least in Rome, the cult of the sun god—either as Apollo or as *sol invictus*, the unconquered sun that appears on the coins of Constantine. Although the Christian presence in Rome was considerable, Mithraism had been all the rage there for some time, and people were wont to ask each other, "Are you for Mithra or for Christ?" It seems that Constantine claimed to have once seen a vision of Apollo, if not of Mithra, and was anxious to keep on the right side of the deities of Rome. What happened to him on his way to attack Maxentius, however, appears to have been of a different order; certainly it was to change his destiny.

There are two phases to the seemingly divine visitation received by Constantine, the first one occurring during the day while he was still in Gaul. He claimed that he saw in the sky a cross, and heard the words, "In this sign thou shalt conquer." Later, the night before his decisive battle with Maxentius, he dreamed of a *chi rho*, a Christian symbol combining of the first two Greek letters of the name of Christ. This may have moved him to have the symbol placed on the shields and standards of his soldiers; since there would not have been time for the armorers to etch or carve it on thousands of shields, it could have been hastily chalked on them. In any case, Constantine attributed his subsequent decisive victory at the Milvian Bridge, where Maxentius made his last stand, to the Christian God. That something about him had changed was evident, and when he entered

Rome he did not offer the traditional victory sacrifices to the Roman gods.

The fateful year 312 saw Constantine become virtual master of the Western Empire—except for one Licinius, a trusted friend of Galerius who had been appointed Augustus of the west in 308, when Constantine's bid was ignored. He too was at odds with Maxentius, and once that rival was out of the way by conveniently dying in the Battle of the Milvian Bridge, Licinius was willing to come to terms with Constantine. They divided the rule of the empire, with Licinius taking the eastern half. They also jointly issued a document proclaiming the right to religious freedom for all citizens of the empire.

This document—popularly known as the Edict of Milan because it was agreed upon there —survives in the copy issued by Licinius in the East, recorded by contemporary Church historians. It was undeniably a historical landmark. The ancient world knew state religions; it did not know the right of citizens to refuse a state religion. A dispensation for Jews had been in effect for centuries, but that was an isolated case, and in spite of their exemption even they occasionally suffered from pagan mobs. The edict, however, stated that every citizen of the empire had the right to worship as he chose; not only that, but the property confiscated both from individual Christians and from the Church during the persecutions was to be restored, with state compensation for the owners of such property. For Christians, the consequences of this document were tremendous: no more anxious, secret worship in catacombs, no more persecution— now great churches could be built above ground, and the faithful could begin the slow work of changing Rome into a Catholic empire.

Two years later, for various reasons, the two rulers fell out again, and after Licinius was defeated by Constantine in 324, he was imprisoned, escaping execution only through the pleas of his wife, who was Constantine's sister. (Constantine had him hanged the following year, though.) Some historians favorable to

Constantine state that Licinius deserved his fate because he persecuted Christians in his half of the empire, which he may have done, though whether for political or religious reasons remains obscure. It has been argued in his favor that it was hardly his fault if some of his political opponents also happened to be Christians, and that his goal was not to persecute but to eliminate rebels and troublemakers. In any case, yet another obstacle to the ambitious emperor's rise to sole power had been neatly eliminated.

Constantine was now in complete control of his realm, and though not a Christian, he favored the growth of the Church and the suppression of heresy. He made lavish gifts to popes and bishops throughout his reign, and gave his mother large sums to bestow on new churches and other Christian works. In 325, with Pope Sylvester I, he convened the Council of Nicaea to settle problems within the Church, notably Arianism. Not a well-educated or intellectually gifted man, he did not quite get the point of the Arian controversy. Arius held that Christ was a creature of God and thus not God's equal, while his young opponent, St. Athanasius, held the true Catholic position that Christ is God, the second Person of the Trinity. This sounds like a clear-cut issue, but it was not to Constantine, as is shown by the letter he wrote to both Arius and Athanasius in which he advised them, in effect, to shake hands and make up because really the two thought alike and their dispute was trivial—although nothing could have been further from the truth. (Later, possibly, the emperor did see the point of the Donatist heresy in Africa, since he gave his support to the council and the churchmen who fought the Donatists.)

A New, Christian Rome

Constantine seems to have felt called to build a shining new Christian capital, and his great city of Constantinople (he originally called it New Rome) was consecrated in 330; it would not, however, have the future he had hoped for it. Originally the capital of a Latin empire, it became first Hellenized, because it lay in the midst of a Greek-speaking region, then increasingly isolated from the West, which fell to barbarian invasion, then the capital of a schismatic Greek Orthodox state, and finally the capital of the Ottoman Turks. For over a thousand years, however, Constantinople—or Byzantium, its original Greek name—would be the center of both Eastern Christian thought and classical Greek culture. While barbarians took over the whole of the Western empire, pillaging and destroying much of what the Romans had built over the centuries, civilized life in Constantinople went more or less serenely on. When in the fifth century a barbarian chief ruled from Rome itself, the Eastern capital still had a civilized successor of Constantine on the throne.

Thus much was saved that was lost in the West, but there were also grave defects in the Byzantine system. The Church of the Eastern empire came more and more under the control of the state, an arrangement referred to as caesaro-papism, which would be passed on to other Eastern states converted to Byzantine Christianity, such as Russia. Heresies sprouted when an emperor or empress espoused and promulgated some novel theological idea. The Church in the East still answered to the pope in Rome, but he was so far away and often so weak, hemmed in by barbarians and trying to cope with the other ills of the crumbling Western empire, that his influence in the east waned. Then in 1054 there occurred the Great Schism, which still separates the Orthodox and Catholic churches. Constantine would have been horrified—and perhaps would have thought twice about moving his capital to Byzantium.

The move may have been beneficial for the Church, however. For no matter how tiresome the barbarians became, in the crumbling Rome of St. Peter there was no emperor to try to treat the Church as a department of the state, or to force heresy upon his subjects. *Ubi Petrus, ibi Ecclesia:* "Where Peter is, there is the Church," and the heart of the Church would always be in Rome. Even when the popes had to flee for their lives, they always returned to Peter's city.

Politics and Crimes

Between the Milvian Bridge and the building of his dream city, what of Constantine's personal life and, above all, his religion? As to the former, he was far from a model Christian or even an ordinary one. The excuse that he was not yet baptized hardly excuses the atrocious crimes he committed. Even pagans were shocked at some of the emperor's deeds, though it must be said that his predecessors had certainly provided him with precedent.

Leaving aside his cruelty to the captives he took in his wars against barbarians—they were thrown to the animals in the arenas to entertain the crowds of spectators—there are the sad destinies of those who were closest to the great man. The fate of his father-in-law, Maximian, and that of Licinius, we have already seen. Worse still were those of his wife, Fausta, who may have saved his life when her father wished to eliminate him, and of his first-born son, Crispus, whom he had with his first wife, Minervina. Whether Minervina died or was divorced by Constantine when he wished to make the more advantageous match with Fausta, the daughter of an Augustus, we do not know, though by all accounts his attitude toward the son he had with Minervina was that of an affectionate father. Constantine gave Crispus a renowned Christian scholar, Lactantius, for his tutor, and later entrusted the young man with military and naval missions in which he supported his father ably and earned the affection of his men. In due course, Crispus married and had a son of his own—apparently to his father's great delight. Yet Constantine later turned against his son and eventually had him killed.

Why? This is the question that has baffled, indeed maddened, historians for the last 1,600 years or so. Why was this talented young man, clearly qualified to be a worthy heir to his father, suddenly put on trial—for an unknown offense—and executed on his father's order? Theories abound; evidence does not. The fact that his stepmother Fausta shared his fate—possibly more gruesomely—a few months later has generated speculation that the two cases were somehow connected. Some said that Fausta knew of an illicit affair in which Crispus was engaged, and which would have outraged the strict moral sense of his father, and told Constantine of it. Others said that Fausta was jealous of Crispus, who stood in the way of her own sons' succession, and therefore accused Crispus of plotting his father's overthrow. Still another story holds that Fausta falsely accused Crispus of attempting to seduce her, and violently. There is no evidence for any of these theories, though it seems likely that Constantine would believe any tale that Fausta told him; had she not revealed to him her own father's plans to kill him?

After what, despite its legal trappings, can only be called the murder of Crispus, a reaction must have set in. Perhaps someone proved to Constantine that whatever Fausta had told him was false, and he went mad with remorse at what he had done. Perhaps it was his mother, Helena, heartsick over the whole affair, who convinced him that he had been wrong. Some such reaction would tend to explain why his next victim was Fausta herself. We do not know whether she was guilty, but in any case she was murdered in her bath. The Romans were fond of elaborate baths, and the bathrooms of the wealthy had hot water piped into them. If you wished to scald your victim to death, you simply waited until he was splashing about in his tub, locked the door, and saw to it that the boilers in the basement were heated to boiling point. Alternatively, such hot steam could be produced in a steam room that the victim suffocated; if he managed to survive, you sent someone in to stab him. Fausta perished in one of these ways.[2]

It is often said that Helena, at the age of around eighty, made her famous pilgrimage to the Holy Land following the executions of Crispus and Fausta, in expiation for her son's sins and

---

[2] Michael Grant ably summarizes the various possible explanations for these tragedies in his *Constantine the Great*, pp.109-115.

to beg forgiveness for him, though we have no precise information as to the year. Since the accession of her son, Helena had been greatly honored: Constantine gave her the title of Augusta (Empress), had coins struck with her image, named cities after her, and provided her with large sums to spend on charities and churches. It is likely that he also sought her advice on many questions, though if he did so in the Crispus and Fausta affairs he must have disregarded it. Helena's pilgrimage may have been her son's suggestion, a means of obtaining his forgiveness by means of the work of his saintly mother. Whoever suggested it, it became far more than a pilgrimage.

Helena had an inquiring mind and was anxious to find in Palestine the actual sites of the events in the Gospels. Nearly 300 years had passed since the days of Christ, and although many shrines were still kept up and holy sites venerated, the passing centuries had ensured that many others were buried under construction and rubble. Helena paid attention to local traditions and had excavations made on the sites of the holiest events in Christian history, particularly the places of the Crucifixion and Resurrection of our Lord. She also had churches built on the holy sites so that their locations would be permanently marked and brought many precious relics with her when she returned. History owes her a debt of gratitude, which is undiminished by the possibility that some of her information may have been faulty. Biblical archaeology has continued its investigations in the wake of Helena's crews of diggers, ever seeking more data on the holy sites of the biblical lands.

Achievements, Death—and a Baptism Controversy

Despite the blots on his record, Constantine left the empire better than he found it. The Edict of Milan had not merely decreed religious liberty for Romans but had ordered the property confiscated from Christians returned to them. He made some attempt at promulgating laws that conformed to Christian principles, although many harsh and cruel ones remained. He abolished crucifixion and tried to eliminate the gladiator contests. Sunday he declared a day of rest (calling it the "Sun Day" to appeal to pagans). Other measures favored the poor, widows and orphans, and even the liberation of slaves. He promoted and financed many institutions of the Church, from churches to monasteries to charitable foundations, and afforded a degree of security and peace that allowed them to flourish. As Norman H. Baynes put it in his history of Byzantine civilization, even in his new Christian capital of Constantinople, Constantine "could not, of course make Christianity the religion of the Roman State—that was unthinkable—but the man to whom the Christian God had amazingly shown unmerited favor had a vision of what in the future might be realized and he could build for the future. Within the pagan empire itself one could begin to raise another—a Christian—empire: and one day the walls of the pagan empire would fall and in their place the Christian building would stand revealed."[3]

This is the lasting glory of Constantine the Great, one of the founders of that Christendom that came out of the disintegration of the western part of his Roman Empire little more than a century after he was gone. His fostering of Catholic institutions and evangelization ensured that even in his lifetime the faith was spread within and beyond the boundaries of Rome. Barbarian regions, from the further shores of the Black Sea to the lands of the uncivilized masses to the north and east of the Roman borders, would hear the good news for the first time. We will trace the stories of some of those areas in later chapters, but for now it is enough to recognize that Constantine's liberation of the Church was a seminal factor in their conversions.

In due course, even the life of such an oversized and powerful figure must come to an end. Constantine died in 337, apparently a Catholic—but when was he baptized? The question is simple,

---

[3] Baynes and Moss, p. xviii.

but the answer is maddeningly elusive. Nearly all authorities accept the account of Eusebius of Caesarea, a contemporary historian who probably got it from Eusebius, bishop of Nicomedia, who was said to have performed the rite on the dying emperor. There are a few problems with this, aside from the fact that Eusebius was an Arian and hardly an ideal choice to baptize an emperor who had a role in condemning Arianism. Furthermore, are we to think that throughout his long reign during which he promoted Christianity, Constantine did not join the Church, never received Holy Communion or absolution for his sins in sacramental confession, or indeed any other sacrament—that he never became a true member of the community he fostered and patronized?

It is true that at the time people sometimes delayed their sacraments of initiation until the approach of death to be sure that *all* their sins were wiped away and there was little risk of committing any more before entering eternity. The majority verdict of historians is that Constantine was such a person. He certainly had enough on his conscience to make him fear for his future behavior and therefore wish to get baptized at a time when further murders, for example, would be impossible to commit.

And yet there is the mute testimony of that obelisk in Rome.

In front of the ancient archbasilica of St. John Lateran, official seat of the pope and the ancient baptistery of Rome, there stands an Egyptian obelisk. Constantine had found the thing in Egypt and intended to bring it to Constantinople, though he only got it as far as Alexandria. After his death, one of his sons had it brought instead to Rome, and by the late 16th century it had made its way to the front of the city's oldest basilica. On the base of this obelisk is an inscription stating plainly that Constantine was baptized in St. John Lateran by Pope St. Sylvester I, who reigned from 314 to 335 (the longest reign up to that time since that of St. Peter). It was Constantine who gave the Lateran Palace—formerly called, ironically, the house of Fausta in the days when her husband still loved her—to the papacy, and it was Pope Sylvester who dedicated the Lateran Palace and the adjacent basilica in 324. The obelisk inscription is undated, but certainly it supports the Roman tradition of Constantine's baptism there, and there is no question that he and Pope Sylvester knew each other.

Furthermore, Constantine was an emotional and impulsive man. When, as he believed, the Christian God had given him signs of favor and led him to victory in his decisive and crucial battle, was the emperor likely to refuse to enter the Church of that God? We are asked to believe, in effect, that whenever the thought of baptism occurred to him, Constantine would coldly and rationally tally up the sins he was still likely to commit before he died and put the thing off. Repeatedly. It is hard to imagine his beloved and respected mother giving him such advice, and it does not seem to fit the mentality of a man who was neither a calculating reasoner nor a habitual procrastinator.

So, if he had really been baptized in Rome soon after the Battle of the Milvian Bridge, what are we to make of the alleged deathbed baptism in Nicomedia? Bishop Eusebius might have had his own reasons for claiming the distinction and glory of baptizing the illustrious emperor; perhaps he hoped it would increase Arianism's battered prestige. Is it possible that what he administered was not in fact a baptismal rite, but absolution after a general confession, extreme unction, and Viaticum? For if the Roman obelisk inscription were false, why was it never corrected or removed? Perhaps we will know the truth of the matter someday.

Church and State after Constantine

Instead we enter a period of see-sawing on the part of Constantine's imperial successors that reflected the still somewhat volatile situation of Roman society. The varying fortunes of the Altar of Victory, a goddess-statue that was a fixture in the Roman senate chamber, is a sort of metaphor for the ups and downs of pagan-Christian rivalries and tensions. This altar was installed by

Octavian, who took the name of Augustus following his victory over the forces of Antony and Cleopatra at the Battle of Actium in 31 B.C., and who as first emperor of Rome went on to a long history of presiding over senatorial affairs.

During the reigns of Constantine's successors, Christian senators began to complain about the pagan altar, and Constantine's son, Emperor Constantius II, had it removed. This did not please the pagan senators, and under Constantius's successor, Julian the Apostate, the thing was hauled back into the senate chamber. Julian had a very brief reign, and once he blew over the Christian senators again campaigned for the altar's removal. The Emperor Gratian (375-383) had it evicted once more in 382, but the pagans were not reconciled to its loss, and two years later the pagan prefect of Rome, Symmachus, petitioned the Emperor Valentinian II for the return of the altar. The case is noteworthy because of the entrance of St. Ambrose of Milan into the fray. He argued strongly against the return of the pagan altar, and Symmachus lost the battle of words. Still, the pagans were not quite finished. One last time, somewhere in the 390s, a usurper who briefly took over the imperial throne restored the altar, after which the issue disappears from history, as no doubt the altar also did in the fifth century, when Rome became more solidly Christian.

Although it is somewhat comical to picture pagans and Christians alternately forming work gangs to transport a huge piece of statuary in and out of the senate, the controversy signified something much deeper. The pagans, feeling themselves beleaguered by the increased Christianization of their country, their city, and their whole culture, adopted the cause of Victory as a symbol around which they could rally. The Christians likewise came to see the issue as one reflecting the triumph or defeat of the faith in Rome. That the struggle could drag on for close to half a century shows the persistence and militancy of paganism, and it mirrors the alternations in Roman government after Constantine between Christian and pagan control.

The Last Pagan Emperor

Despite the brevity of his reign, it was Julian the Apostate who posed the most serious threat to the triumph of the faith after Constantine. This conflicted young man was the last of the line of Constantine, the son of his half-brother. He was raised a Christian and studied in Constantinople, Nicomedia, and Athens, where he became fascinated with mystical neo-Platonism as well as with paganism. He was drawn to some sort of spirituality but seems to have abandoned Christianity for a variety of rather lame reasons: members of his family had perished in the political upheavals that followed the death of Constantine, and those who killed them were Christians; one of his teachers had changed his religion several times; another prophesied that Julian would someday restore paganism. In any case, by the age of 20 Julian would famously proclaim his position on Christianity: "I have read, I have understood, I have rejected."

On his accession to power in 360, he re-opened the pagan temples, restored sacrifices (and offered them himself), and rewarded apostates. When Christians resisted and protested the confiscation of churches that had once been temples, Julian went further. Christians were barred from teaching positions; pagan mobs, eager for victory over their hated opponents, sacked churches and murdered Christians, even torturing to death a bishop who had once saved Julian's life. Anti-Christian polemics spread, fueled by the emperor's own anti-Christian writings. Julian even set out to rebuild the temple of Jerusalem as an act of defiance of Christ's prophecy that not one stone of the temple would be left upon another. Repeated attempts at restoration failed, foiled by earthquake and—more than once—by mysterious fire that came out of the ground and destroyed the builders' tools (and nearly the builders, too).

Fortunately for the Church, Julian had only two years in office to try to stamp out the religion of his youth, dying while on campaign against the Persians at the age of 32. (There seems no evidence that his last words were "Galilean, thou hast conquered," an admission often attributed to him.) He seems to have been a thoroughly nasty and unbalanced young man, though his biographers and other historians tend to fall under his spell and find themselves making excuses for him. Even Abbot Ricciotti, in his biography of the ill-fated emperor, concludes: "No one today would call Julian into court for his apostasy. This was a matter for his own conscience, and was in large measure provoked by the misfortunes that befell his relatives and by the friendships he formed at Ephesus and Athens."[4] Henri Daniel-Rops also finds some excuse for him: "Julian erred in his means, but his intentions were noble. Observing the frightful disintegration of the ancient world, he decided that Christianity was responsible, and by suppressing it he would be eliminating a fatal leaven. Here he was misguided."[5]

Oh. Well, if he was misguided, the poor man, perhaps we ought to excuse his youthful errors.

After Julian, the emperors of both the Eastern and Western empires would be Christians—sometimes wishy-washy Christians, sometimes leaning toward some heresy or other, but anyway they were not pagan. Those days were gone forever. The great conversion of Rome would not be undone, or at least not completely.

The empire's conversion would not progress, however, without significant struggle. Besides Nero, Decius, Diocletian, Julian, and other zealous persecutors, potential converts to Christianity in the Roman world faced many challenges. The world of Rome, particularly late Rome, was something like our own. The old virtues cultivated during the Roman Republic, the ideals of self-control, moderation, and simple living, waned as the empire became urbanized, and the transformation brought many changes to society, creating new and serious obstacles to conversion.

---

4 Ricciotti, p. 258.
5 Daniel-Rops, *The Church of Apostles and Martyrs*, p. 563.

Bread and Circuses

Rome itself had perhaps a million inhabitants, and other large cities several hundred thousand. Those cities contained both rich and poor, with large numbers of the poor constituting a destitute underclass that needed to be fed and entertained by the state. Many of them had flocked to the cities because they had lost farm jobs due mostly to the increasing use of slave labor or to the soil exhaustion that was beginning to plague farmers. Once in the cities, these masses lived in multistory tenements that were provided by the state along with food allowances and entertainment in the huge amphitheaters that were a prominent feature of all sizeable Roman cities.

If their idleness and crowded living conditions tended to coarsen the Roman poor and warp their minds and standards of behavior, the entertainments did so to a much greater degree. Seneca, an educated Stoic thinker, admitted that after viewing one of those shows he felt he had become more dissipated, cruel, even inhuman. They seem to have started as gymnastic and sports competitions in the early Roman period, with chariot racing among the more benign spectacles. But by the late Roman period the shows were mostly violent: wild animals pitted against each other, for instance, or against gladiators. Combats between two gladiators, or between groups of them, were also extremely popular; top gladiators—meaning those who had survived by killing large numbers of opponents—were the film stars of their day. Demand for variety also meant having dwarfs or women, as well as gladiators, fighting to the death, and when the persecutions began, the slow torture of Christians in a variety of ways provided new thrills.

Decline in Morals and Family Life

The mental and spiritual effects that Seneca noted in himself were multiplied in the mobs addicted to a constant diet of such depraved stimulation. The individuals that made up such mobs were hardly likely—barring a miracle, and, of course, miracles did happen—to be receptive to the doctrines and moral principles of Christianity. In fact, the morals of late Rome had suffered a disastrous decline when compared with the morality of the Roman Republic and even the early empire. In early Rome, the family had been a precious institution, the backbone of the state, with marriage as its linchpin. The name for citizen, in fact, was *paterfamilias,* or "father of a family," an honorable title. The mother was similarly honored, with many stories in Roman literature of the virtue and nobility of Roman matrons. Children were valued, as the story of the widow Cornelia, mother of the Gracchi brothers, illustrates. It was said that when a tyrant summoned her and demanded that she turn over her jewels, she called her 12 children around her and proudly declared to the bully: "These are my jewels."

By late Roman times, women were no longer anxious to bear children (we know they practiced abortion and contraception), and marriages ended in easy divorce with increasing frequency. At the other extreme, we read complaints from Roman writers of this period about children being badly spoiled and undisciplined. Teenagers were given too much money and spent it recklessly, leading to dissipation of both wealth and morals. Since the Romans had placed the family at the heart of their state as it was originally founded, this disintegration of the Roman family had serious consequences for Rome itself.

It should also be recalled that Rome—like most ancient civilizations—was a slave society. In the beginning, most Romans were small farmers with a small number of slaves to help them in the fields and in the house. We find these slaves referred to as "family," and it seems they were in general decently treated. They could be tutors to children, or their escorts to and from school, and hold other responsible positions, and could buy their freedom or be freed by their masters. In later centuries, a large influx of slaves occurred due to imperial military campaigns that brought masses of prisoners of war back to Italy. These enslaved foreigners were often used in large numbers to work the mines or the plantations in the south of the peninsula, under the supervision of brutal overseers. Their conditions were so bad that slave revolts sometimes occurred; they were always suppressed, usually with great cruelty. Seneca and other Stoics argued for humane treatment of slaves, on the grounds that slaves were just as human as their masters, but the coarser Roman life became, the less interested Romans were in making things easier for their slaves.

Barbarians at the Border

By the third, fourth, and fifth centuries, grave dangers threatened the existence of the Roman world as barbarians increasingly pushed on the borders from all directions. It is hard to imagine that for several centuries Rome maintained border defenses from Britain to Mesopotamia and across North Africa, crisscrossed by 53,000 miles of those famous Roman roads—some of them still in use today. The conquered areas of the empire became Roman provinces, often with a degree of self-government, and benefited from imperial protection and trade. By the third century, migrations of tribes beyond the borders led to an increasing number of enemy incursions. This required military spending beyond the citizens' ability to provide, but the tax-gatherers, particularly under Diocletian, were merciless. The taxpayers became increasingly servants of the state, fixed in their professions or tied to the land they rented so the tax-gatherer would know where to find them.

Corruption of Culture

In the cultural sphere, by the fourth and fifth centuries things were going downhill pretty fast. The glories of "golden" Latin and "silver" Latin, referring to periods during the republic and early empire when the Latin literary masterpieces were produced, were far in the past. The language had become debased, as fewer and fewer Romans cared to cultivate good style and correct grammar. Jargon and slang were common, and illiteracy was increasing. Art and architecture became more flamboyant and exaggerated, compared with the purity of style and clean lines of classical buildings and structures.

Even the old Roman religion changed for the worse. In the early Roman period, we find the worship of one god, Jupiter, apparently brought by the Italic tribes when they migrated into Italy, who was the king of all other gods there might happen to be. The Romans were also attached to the numerous spirits they thought to be involved in every aspect of life—they were convinced, for example, that some spirit presided over the seed they planted in the soil, that another was involved in the growth of the stalk, and still another in the formation of the fruit. There were spirits—*abeona* and *adeona*—who presided over a child's first steps away from its mother and its first steps back. In later ages, Romans adopted the gods of Greece and of various other cultures, from Egypt to Persia, but the sense of an intimate spiritual universe seems to have stayed with them to some extent. By the late empire, however, rulers themselves were claiming to be gods and demanding worship, while secret—often very unpleasant—mystical cults proliferated; all of this, of course, was wholly inimical to Christianity.

Heresy and Sorcery

For anyone interested in converting to Christianity in the ancient world, as indeed for centuries to come, many sinister factors helped complicate his choice. The proliferation of heresies meant that it was by no means easy for a would-be convert to discern just which of the many sects within the Roman Empire was the true religion, if there was a true religion in the first place. One formidable rival to Christianity was the Manichaean sect to which St. Augustine belonged for a time. This weird dualistic religion originated in Persia. Its founder, Mani, was a third-century Persian who seems to have wanted to unite the elements of all the world's religions in his new system. Manichaeism was to have a long life in the West, and in the East as far as China. In the 12th and 13th centuries we will meet it in various parts of southern Europe, particularly the south of France, where it occasioned the Albigensian Crusade. The Manichees professed a dualism according to which matter was evil and symbolized by darkness, and spirit was good, symbolized by light. It stressed salvation through reason and knowledge, though its many doctrines had to be taken on faith. There was god of good, a god of evil, and several other gods or semi-gods, as well as other characters in its mythology. It also came to include elements of the various religions with which the Manicheans came in contact; these familiar elements appealed to adherents of those religions, who could gradually be converted to Mani's new faith.

Ironically, Manicheans sometimes claimed to be also Christians; whether or not that was Diocletian's reason for persecuting them, it became a long-lasting policy of the emperors, both pagan and Christian, to try to stamp out the sect. Whatever its attraction, it made Manicheans of numerous ordinary people as well as sophisticated intellectuals such as Augustine, before his conversion.[6] We will see examples of the bizarre Manichean way of life when we get to the Cathars in chapter 6.

Of course, Christianity had from the start been plagued by heresies, particularly in the Greek-speaking part of the empire. Arius, a sophisticated priest, started a notorious one, mentioned earlier, in Egypt, and it won many powerful adherents. Even when Arianism was condemned at the Council of Nicaea and the doctrine of the Trinity firmly proclaimed in the Nicene Creed, the Arians were not finished; their missionaries went outside the boundaries of Rome to various barbarian tribes whom they converted, which is a story for a later chapter.

If you were looking for religious truth in the Roman Empire, then, you might have investigated (and, we hope, rejected) Manichaeism and Arianism. What was left, apart from the Church itself, besides other heresies such as that of the Donatists? Many

---

6 Arendzen, "Manichæism," *The Catholic Encyclopedia* vol. 9.

(perhaps most) Romans were convinced that there was an occult world that just might satisfy their spiritual thirst. It is difficult for us to imagine the role of magicians and sorcerers in the ancient world, but they were certainly there. Simon Magus, who appears in the book of Acts as a magician who tried to buy additional magical powers from the apostles, is one example of this category of magic practitioners. They were not merely tricksters, like our performers at magic shows. They claimed occult powers and were described in many reputable sources as actually performing what seemed to be miracles. Lactantius, the Christian scholar and tutor of Constantine's son Crispus, wrote that the magicians of his day indeed performed wonders, only not on the order of those Christ had done. No magician ever came back from the dead, but their feats were certainly sensational enough, and we will see them turning up for centuries, dogging the steps of Christian missionaries throughout Europe. Lactantius attributed their powers to demons; perhaps Satan was waging a desperate struggle to prevent the religion of Christ from making conversions anywhere.

We must not forget, finally, that the whole of late Roman culture and society, as mentioned above, was permeated with pagan ideas and customs, with its landscapes and cityscapes filled with pagan temples, shrines, and places sacred to some god or other. If you became a Christian in those times and were asked to dinner by a neighbor, how could you avoid giving the traditional greeting to his household gods, or pouring a libation of wine to them? How could you send your children to Roman schools, where paganism permeated the curriculum? You could hardly work for the government, since that required acts of homage to the gods, nor could you be an actor and portray immoral behavior on the stage. Thus, the very nature of pagan Roman society meant that you would have to exclude yourself from many ordinary and customary activities within it. You would become an outsider and perhaps thereby draw unwelcome attention to yourself and your family.

Given the tremendous obstacles to conversion posed by Roman culture and society, as well as the competition of heresies, sects, and sorcerers, it is a miracle in itself that somehow the whole Roman world did, in fact, convert. We will be following that progress north, east, and west from Rome in the chapters to follow.

———————

Had the conversion of the empire not occurred, it is hard to see how the rest of Europe—and hence the rest of the world—would ever have been evangelized. Possibly a Christianity restricted to the eastern Mediterranean littoral would have been able to extend through the Middle East and parts of Africa, but the West would have remained under the sway of the pagan and occult forces that dominated it until its conversion. Rome, then, was key. Its roads, universal languages (Hellenistic Greek and/or Latin), its urban environment, the peace and order it imposed, even its mild climate—all these factors facilitated the transmission of the faith throughout the empire and made Rome the headquarters for the adventurous missions that the Church would send to the corners of the earth.

ℬ Instruments of Conversion ℭ

Oral Preaching and Witness

Only rarely does God manifest himself to a person he wants to convert, as he did to St. Paul; in most cases he makes use of human instruments. These will differ according to time, place, and other circumstances.

In the case of the Roman Empire, the primary instrument of conversion was the spoken word. It is often hard for us to imagine to what extent the civilization of the ancient world was based on oral transmission and therefore on memorization. The literate Greeks of the Classical Age possessed books, but they also committed to memory classics such as the tales of Homer, a feat that we moderns, with our atrophied memories and our dependence on the written word, cannot fathom. It was the same with the Jews, who certainly had libraries with copies of their sacred books but who also taught their children to memorize those books. It was the same with the Gospels, which were first transmitted orally. Likewise, when a letter from St. Paul arrived in a city, it was read aloud and committed to memory by the listeners for further transmission until the precious words could be copied and sent further afield.

In the early days of our story, then, we find the faith spreading primarily by word of mouth among the illiterate as well as the literate. To this oral preaching was joined stories of the example of Christian living, so much at odds with the decadence of the Roman Empire. "See the Christians, how they love one another!" the pagans marveled, and found themselves attracted to such a way of life. As the persecutions began in the first century and increased in number and severity over the next 200 years, news of these Christians who endured such suffering and death for their God moved many Romans to consider the claims of the new religion.

Gaul : 3rd-8th century A.D.

SALIAN FRANKS
early 5th century

Reims
● St. Remigius, 397✝

Attila the Hun
XX 451

Paris
● St. Gertrude c.512✝

Tours
● St. Martin, 397✝

Poitiers
● XX Martel vs. Moors 732

Lyon
Ireneus, bishop, 202✝

Apt ●

2

The Eldest Daughter of the Church

The conversion of Gaul has an importance beyond the evangelization of yet another Roman province, important as that was. The destiny of Catholic France was to be of paramount importance for Western history. When Rome had fallen to barbarian invaders, the slow emergence of a new Catholic civilization took place in northwestern Europe, mostly in France. It would be largely the French, many of them saints, who would produce the institutions, sacred art and architecture, schools, universities, and renewed urban culture, all of them of Catholic inspiration, that would eventually bring a renaissance to the former provinces of Rome and lay the foundations of European Christendom.

There was a Christian presence in the Roman province of Gaul, the future France, from the earliest Christian era—at least in the cities. The Roman Empire was thoroughly urban, and the Church likewise functioned mainly in the urban areas. Whereas during the Republican era Romans of all classes had lived mostly on the land, things were quite different in the citified empire. Wealthy Romans might still have country estates, but they also had townhouses, since everything of interest and importance happened in the growing imperial cities. Men seeking careers in government, business, or cultural institutions such as the Roman schools naturally gravitated to the cities. Many of the key events recounted in the Gospels and in Acts occurred within those city walls. St. Paul traveled from town to city to seaport in his missionary journeys, and so did those who followed him in spreading the faith.

In the eastern part of the empire, where town and country were closely linked commercially and geographically, the evangelization of country dwellers could go hand in hand with that of the neighboring towns. In the Western empire, however, particularly in the increasingly unstable era we are entering—the third, fourth, and fifth centuries—things were not so simple. Romans built cities everywhere they went or enlarged the native towns, but in the more distant provinces they were few and far between. The majority of the subject populations lived in the country and often had little contact with their new political masters. Unlike Roman city dwellers, those rural inhabitants were often uneducated, even illiterate, and they did not share the common cultural background that made it easy for Christians to converse with pagans in Roman cities.

In the northern and western provinces of Rome, country dwellers thought in categories unfamiliar to classically trained apostles; they could not even be counted on to speak Latin or Greek, so their barbaric tongues had to be mastered. (The very word *barbarian* may have come from the perception that the ancient Greeks had of such foreigners: to Greek ears their language sounded like "bar bar bar.") This necessity of learning barbarian tongues and dialects was a daunting one. Already in the second century St. Irenaeus, the great theologian born in Asia Minor who later became bishop of Lyon in Gaul, remarked that he had to speak Celtic to some of his converts.

Then there was the problem of barbarian religions. Except for the tribes who were converted to Arianism or some other sect of Roman origin, these country dwellers lived in an alien spiritual world governed by magical practices, sects such as the Druids and their priests and the ever-present influence of sorcerers and soothsayers. No wonder it was quite a while after sizeable Christian communities had developed in the urban centers of the empire that we hear of successful attempts to evangelize the countryside. And in the Late Roman period, the future states of Western Europe were largely composed of countryside.

Early Christianity in Gaul

Some of the earliest Christian communities mentioned in surviving documents were based in the cities of Lyon and Vienne in Gaul. A letter sent by the Christians of these two cities to

Christian communities in Asia describes a vicious persecution, probably the one that began in 177. The original perpetrators of the violence were not Roman government officials but mobs of townspeople who attacked their Christian neighbors and caused such a disturbance that their victims were hauled before the local authorities. Among them was the bishop of Lyon, St. Pothinus, then in his 90s, who was so badly abused that he died in prison after two days of suffering. St. Irenaeus, who was a priest of Lyon at the time, escaped this persecution. He had been sent to Rome with a letter for the pope, and upon his return, he succeeded Pothinus as bishop.

When those who had been rounded up admitted to being Christians, they were imprisoned until the governor arrived, interrogated again, and summoned to renounce their faith. According to the letter, about 10, who "appeared unprepared and untrained and still weak, unable to endure the strain of a great contest," became apostates. This shook the rest of the group, causing them "great pain and excessive sorrow, and weakened the zeal of the others who had not yet been seized." A few pagan servants of some of the Christians, who had been rounded up with them, agreed to accuse them falsely of abominable behavior to save their own skins; this aroused the mob and the officials to fury, and the fate of the prisoners was sealed.

In the detailed account that we have from the Church historian Eusebius, four of the martyrs are singled out as particularly enraging the mob; three of them were apparently pillars of the Christian community and brave confessors of the faith, but the fourth was a poor, weak slave girl named Blandina. Despite her frailty, her captors "took turns in torturing her in every manner from dawn till evening and they confessed that they were defeated and had nothing more which they could do to her. They marveled at her endurance, for her whole body was mangled and broken; and they testified that one form of torture was sufficient to destroy life, to say nothing of so many and so great tortures."

The authorities agreed to give the mob a day's "entertainment" of watching these four heroes tortured in ingenious ways, apparently according to suggestions proposed by the crowd in the amphitheater. The appalling acts of this sacred drama included attacks by wild beasts and roasting the men in iron chairs so that the stench of their burning flesh hung over the crowd; it seems their sufferings lasted an entire day. Blandina was suspended on a pole in the arena for the beasts, yet she continuously encouraged the men throughout their ordeal. None of the beasts would touch her, so she was again imprisoned. At last, the remaining Christians were again brought before the governor and ordered to apostatize and be set free, or else to die by beheading (a mercy reserved for Roman citizens) or by the beasts. At that point, even some who had apostatized earlier retracted and died bravely. As for Blandina, having suffered still more tortures, she was tied into a net to be tossed by bulls, which finally caused her death.

The bodies of the martyrs were destroyed and their ashes thrown into the river so that no relics might remain. "Now let us see," the pagans sneered, "whether they will rise again."[7]

Thus the blood of martyrs watered the soil of France, soil that would bring forth some of the greatest Catholic rulers and saints in all of history. Not just yet, however.

Of St. Anne, St. Lazarus, and St. Mary Magdalene

Before we get to the later periods of conversion and the flourishing of the Church in peace, we should pay some attention to an ancient French tradition linking the presence of Christianity in Gaul to the time immediately following the Ascension of our Lord—hence, to the first half of the first century A.D. The accounts on which this tradition is based state that when the Jews began persecuting Christians after the Resurrection, St. Mary

---

7 Perry, *Sources*, pp. 177-179.

Magdalene and her brother Lazarus left Palestine for the western Mediterranean to help spread the gospel there. Fearing for the fate of the tomb of St. Anne, our Lady's mother, they took her remains with them to re-inter in their new home in the town of Apt in southern France. St. Maximin, one of the 72 helpers of the apostles, was in the group that accompanied them, and he later became the bishop of Apt. Others (such as Mary's sister Martha) are sometimes mentioned in other texts. Once in Gaul, Mary Magdalene devoted most of her remaining years to prayer and penance in a cave or grotto now known as Sainte-Baume, which is still a place of pilgrimage.

This story has been generally dismissed as legend, though there is nothing inherently fantastic about it. Many people traveled long distances within the Roman Empire, either on the excellent roads or the busy sea routes of the Mediterranean. The shores of southern France had long been known to soldiers, traders, and other travelers, and the mild climate resembled that of Palestine. The travelers had a good chance of being safe from persecution there, and certainly there was scope for spreading the good news.

So far the tale is not at all unlikely, but what is the evidence that it is true?

Recent scholars have examined early medieval accounts of this saga and traced their sources back as far as the fifth century. Excavations made in the 1990s have uncovered the remains of a church that existed prior to the Lombard incursions of the sixth century, a church that tradition links with the tomb of Mary Magdalene. There is more support for this thesis than for the location of St. Anne's remains, though there is a reliquary of her in St. Anne's cathedral at Apt.

Research into the authenticity of all these remains is complicated by the fact that some of them had to be moved more than once to be hidden from invaders. The Cathedral of Vezelay long claimed to possess Mary Magdalene's remains and might actually have done so for a time when they were moved there for safekeeping. What remains of her tomb, however, does seem to be in Apt.[8]

All this is related, whether historically or mythically, to the presence of the Church and its missionaries in Gaul in the earliest Christian period.

St. Martin: Convert-Maker of Gaul

What we know of St. Martin comes primarily from the account of his life written by Sulpicius Severus, who became Martin's disciple as well as his biographer. Sulpicius is an interesting example of the cultivation of classical learning in the fourth and early fifth centuries, in at least some of the Roman provinces—in this case, Aquitania in southern Gaul. He was born into a noble Roman family, received a good education, and became a lawyer and writer. It is unclear whether the family was Christian or pagan, but Sulpicius became a major Christian writer of his day. His friend, St. Paulinus of Nola, of similar background, influenced Sulpicius in favor of the monastic life that was beginning to take hold in Gaul. Already, early in Christian history, we find complaints about the worldliness of some of the secular clergy and hierarchy, and fervent souls were drawn to a more perfect religious life. Martin, by the time he met Sulpicius, had felt the same attraction to monasticism.

Martin was born to a Roman military family at Savaria in the province of Pannonia, in today's town of Szombathély, Hungary, in about 315. His parents were pagans, though Martin seems to have become a catechumen at a young age, possibly while the family was stationed in Italy. (The Edict of Milan had been issued by Constantine and Licinius three years earlier, making Christianity legal.) As the son of a soldier, Martin was required

---

8   The Catholic writer Frances Parkinson Keyes became interested in the St. Anne story and wrote a fine biography of the saint, *St. Anne, Grandmother of Our Saviour,* in which she argues persuasively for the veracity of the Apt tradition.

to follow that profession. He joined a cavalry unit while still a teenager and was sent to Gaul, where, in what is now the city of Amiens, the famous episode of the cloak occurred. At the gates of the city he met a poor beggar suffering from the cold. Moved by compassion, Martin cut a piece from his cloak and gave it to the man. That night he dreamed he saw Jesus wearing the cloak, and according to Sulpicius he heard Jesus say to the angels: "Here is Martin, the Roman soldier who is not baptized; he has clothed me."

This dream, or vision, made a profound impression on Martin. He had been a catechumen for three years and now, at the age of 18, he requested baptism. His new ambition was to be not a Roman soldier but a soldier of Christ. Around 336 his unit was ordered into battle near the Rhine. Martin refused, apparently claiming that his religion prevented him from fighting. (If he really said this he was in error, since the Church had never condemned military service, and many Christians served in the Roman army.) He was charged with cowardice and imprisoned, whereupon he changed course and volunteered to lead his men into battle, at their head and unarmed. Before he could be taken up on this interesting offer, the enemy came to terms, and Martin was allowed to resign.

What was he to do now? He first went to the Roman town that is now Tours, where he became a disciple of St. Hilary of Poitiers, the great champion of Catholic doctrine against the Arianism that was spreading even within imperial court circles. With this learned and humble saint, Martin studied theology and made such progress that Hilary wanted to ordain him. Martin vehemently refused; he was going to imitate the Desert Fathers and that was that. His clever mentor tried a different approach: What if Martin were to receive only one of the minor orders, that of exorcist? When Martin objected even to this, Hilary managed to suggest that his refusal might be motivated by pride; was the minor order too minor for him? Confounded, Martin gave way. He may have feared entering into battle with Satan, but he probably did not foresee how much of his future apostolate would be devoted to bitter combats with the Prince of Darkness.

Before pursuing his vocation further, however, Martin wanted to return home to Pannonia and bring the good news to his parents. We cannot go into the adventures he had along the way, including capture by brigands—whom he converted—and a brief meeting with Satan, who warned him that he would dog his steps for the rest of his life, but at length he arrived at his old home. There he succeeded in leading his mother into the faith, though he was disappointed in his hopes for the conversion of his father. He discovered that Arianism was rife in Pannonia and courageously attacked it, which brought him insults, beatings, and so many obstacles to his preaching that he had to give it up and return to Gaul. Before his arrival, however, he learned that the Arians had succeeded in banishing many orthodox priests, including his old mentor, Hilary. Martin retreated to a rocky Italian island where he lived in solitude until news came of Hilary's return from exile and they met again near Tours.

Now, at 44, Martin determined to be a hermit for good. He started out all right, settling into a hut in a rough, mountainous area and living on water and roots. There he was joined by a pious companion who shared his ideals, and then by a few more. Then something happened that was to be the beginning of a lifelong trial. In Martin's absence one of these companions became ill and died. On his return he raised him to life, and the fat was in the fire. Mobs of the faithful came to get a look at the miracle worker, who already had the reputation of a saint, and when he restored life to another dead man, a slave this time, his fame spread even further. The result was a flood of vocations that led to the foundation of the large and successful monastic community of Marmoutiers.

Soon a large number of pious families were living around the monastery, tilling the soil and learning from the monks. Grace was obviously at work in the souls of these people who were attracted by the monks who had settled among them. Conversions multiplied; a community of nuns was formed not far away. This of course was not at all what Martin had envisaged when he took up the hermit life, but he could hardly be sorry about how it had developed. He finally agreed to ordination as a priest, but even that was not the end of the events that thrust him into a life far removed from that of the Desert Fathers. The See of Tours became vacant and Martin—horrified and protesting in vain— was proposed as the next bishop. When he was chosen, he had to be taken prisoner by his enthusiastic supporters and hauled bodily to the town to be consecrated. He proved to be a great prelate, somehow managing to combine, for the rest of his life (approximately the years 370 to 395), the charisms and duties of bishop, hermit, abbot, and missionary.

At first glance, the goals of monasticism would seem to be at odds with those of evangelization. Monks retire from the world to attend to their souls and to pray day and night. They pray *for* the world, of course, but they do not get involved with it more than necessary. Although this retirement from the world may have been (and still is) a true monastic ideal, not even the Desert Fathers of the third and fourth centuries, who lived mostly as solitary hermits in the Egyptian desert, were able to cut themselves off completely. Time after time some obligation of charity would require them to receive travelers needing help or to leave their cells for the city when some soul was in dire need. Later on we will see something similar happening to the many Benedictine communities that spread throughout the hinterlands of the former Roman Empire. They began by seeking the solitude of the countryside; they ended by opening guesthouses, clinics, and schools for their neighbors and teaching them the faith. Thus it was with poor Martin, who was rarely at home in his beloved cell or even his in his Spartan office in the chancery.

On the several long journeys he had already made, Martin saw that the countryside of Gaul was deeply imbued with paganism. The old Roman gods may have been defeated in the increasingly Christian cities, but the peasants believed the gods

lived on in the forests and the fields. Besides these vestiges of
Roman paganism, indigenous cults and magical practices were
widespread and entrenched in the rural pagan world. Druidism,
for example, flourished in Gaul, Ireland, and Britain, though not
in the German lands. Julius Caesar had written of the Druids in
his account of his campaigns in Gaul in the first century B.C.;
from his writings and those of several other Roman writers, it
appears that the Druids were both a social caste in Celtic society
and leaders of a religious cult that practiced human sacrifice,
believed in reincarnation, and considered some elements of the
natural world—such as oak trees—sacred.

Among the Gallic population, particularly in western Gaul,
devotion to the old Celtic gods still survived, though the Roman conquerors had successfully substituted Roman deities for
them in many areas. Some earlier Christian missionaries had
managed to dethrone the Roman pagan gods, but that only reinforced popular attachment to the old Celtic ones. Henri Ghéon,
whose wonderful biography *St. Martin of Tours* I have used ex-
tensively for this chapter, writes that, in Martin's day, "At least
three-quarters of the country, lacking contact with the Latin and
Christian culture, still adored Teutates, Arduina, Belan, the Sun,
the Thunder, the Earth and the oldest oaks in the great forests."[9]

Martin's missionary life was thus full of harrowing confronta-
tions with paganism in its many forms, behind all of which he,
the exorcist, saw the hand of Satan. There was, for instance, an
ancient tower in the town of Amboise that seems to have been
the sanctuary of some local warrior god. After a successful mission there, Martin left the town after instructing the remaining
monks to see that the tower was destroyed. When he returned
sometime later, there the thing still was, dominating the hori-
zon. The monks pleaded that they could not persuade enough
workers to destroy the tower, whereupon Martin retired to his
cell and spent the night in prayer. According to the eyewitness

---

[9] Ghéon, p. 84.

account of one of the monks, the following day a tremendous storm blew up and destroyed the tower. The incident so impressed the inhabitants that they gave up their pagan attachments for good.

Another miracle for which Martin became famous involved a huge pine tree, dedicated to some Celtic spirit, that stood next to a pagan temple. Martin and his men had destroyed the temple without interference from the silent crowd of locals who were looking on, but when the saint turned to cut down the tree, they protested violently. Martin argued with them: It was only a tree; they had lots of them. Finally one of them proposed that the pagans would cut down the tree themselves if Martin would stand on the spot where it would fall. If his God was so powerful, the man argued, he would save his servant. Martin agreed. He knelt in prayer as the pagans chopped away, tying ropes to the tree so that it would fall where they wanted it to—on top of Martin. As the great trunk hurtled down on him, Martin made the sign of the cross in the air. The tree stopped and began to fall in the opposite direction, where the gaping pagans were standing, but slowly enough that they could get out of the way. The whole region, a pagan stronghold, shortly became one of the most Catholic parts of Gaul.

The pagans were not the only ones Martin evangelized. There were also prisoners languishing in captivity for want of ransom money, and there was the institution of slavery, which Martin would have abolished if he could have. Failing that, he campaigned for donations to ransom prisoners and free slaves and even visited the emperor on behalf of the slaves. Church councils had authorized bishops to pawn even the sacred liturgical vessels for ransom money; St. Cesarius of Arles had done this with all the treasures of his church, and Martin followed his example.

There is much more to tell of this astonishing saint, but we must stop somewhere, and it will be with this: He created the parish system. We take parishes so much for granted that it is hard to believe they did not always exist. Episcopal sees that extended over very large areas, yes, but Martin, as a missionary bishop, was brought up against the problem of what would happen to the local communities he converted once he and his monks were gone. There came to him the idea of organizing these local Christians around a church, with a priest to care for their spiritual needs, and a periodic visitation from their bishop to ensure that all was going well. Thus Catholic Gaul became a region of parishes, centers for worship and teaching, and the system spread throughout Christendom.

Worn out from his prodigious labors, Martin died around the age of 80 and immediately became the most popular saint in France; to his tomb most of the later French saints came to pray, as well as pilgrims from all over the world. Henri Ghéon, who was a soldier in World War I, thought it no coincidence that the war ended on St. Martin's feast day, November 11. The soldier-saint heard the prayers of the soldiers of France.

The Frankish Conquest of Gaul

Throughout the period we have been considering, particularly the fourth and fifth centuries, the Roman Empire was deteriorating in a number of ways. There was economic trouble, agricultural stagnation, high unemployment, political instability, and even pollution: of the air from the fumes of large lead smelters and of human bodies from dietary lead contamination; all these produced insecurity, ill health, and discontent. Many Romans simply gave up on their own society and government: "They prayed God," according to a writer of the day, "to send them the barbarians."

Who were these barbarians who would bring new blood and fresh ideas to the senile empire? They were not the sedentary and peaceful inhabitants of the Roman provinces like the Gallo-Romans whom Martin converted. Rather, they were the restless warrior tribes that had for centuries been pressing on the Roman frontiers, particularly near the Rhine. There were many such tribes—Visigoths, Ostrogoths, Vandals, Saxons, Franks, and others—which had constituted a long-standing headache for a series of Roman emperors. We have seen how Constantine and his father battled them. By the mid-fifth century, these incursions had become more massive and frequent, and Roman border defenses no longer held. This was particularly the case when the defending soldiers were themselves barbarians who had been taken into the Roman army and were now supposed to fight against their own relatives—which they did badly or not at all. Among the tribes that thus broke into Roman territory and occupied it was the tribe of the Salian Franks. It is they who took over Gaul and ruled over the Gallo-Roman population, and we will deal with them shortly. Before we do so, we should meet the strange people who were responsible for the accelerated pressure of the Germanic tribes on the Roman frontiers and who devastated Gaul before the Franks took over.

The Lady and the Hun

The reason for the frantic westward push of so many different peoples into Roman territory in the fifth century was to be found at the other end of the Eurasian continent in Mongolia. When the Huns—fierce Asiatic warriors who rode small, tough steeds capable of great speed and mobility—began, for unknown reasons, to move westward across the steppes of Asia, they came across native tribes, who fled before them. Those tribes pressed on neighbors further west, spreading the tale of the fierceness and ruthlessness of the Huns and sparking more flight; those panicky tribes swept into the Roman Empire, followed by the Huns themselves. The Huns behaved peacefully, at first, until a new leader emerged who had a great ambition: to create a great global empire of which the Roman Empire would be a small part. Attila the Hun was a brilliant man who spoke civilized languages and had lived among the Romans for a time as a hostage. He thus had the opportunity to assess the strengths and weaknesses of his target and drew up a campaign plan that might, had it succeeded, made what was left of the empire into a province of Mongolia.

Attila's personality, strategy, and campaigns cannot detain us here; neither can his famous meeting with Pope St. Leo I that somehow deflected the king of the Huns from carrying out his grand plans.[10] Attila comes into our story here because of his siege of the city of Paris, the future French capital, which plays such a major role in France's conversion and indeed in all of French history. This city, located on the islands and banks of the river Seine, had been an important Roman center from the first century B.C.; Julius Caesar may have made an encampment nearby during his famous campaign against his Gallic Wars, and under later Roman occupation the baths and amphitheater that can still be seen were built, as well as thousands of houses, marketplaces, and temples. The hill now called Montmartre is a reminder of the fanatical persecutions that reached far into the provincial life of Rome's empire: There several Christians were martyred during the persecution of Decius in 250, including St. Denis, bishop of Paris.

Mention of that event brings us to the extraordinary woman who had the first church built in honor of those martyrs. Her name is St. Genevieve, and she proved to be Attila's nemesis. Genevieve was born a few miles from Paris in the early fifth century and died somewhere between 80 and 100 years later. As a young girl, she met St. Germain, bishop of Auxerre, who had been a worldly young Roman official before his conversion and became a zealous and effective prelate after it. Genevieve confided to him her desire to live only for God, and he recognized her as a chosen soul. Upon her parents' death he advised her to go to Paris to live with her godmother, where she became known for holiness and works of charity, and her opinions seem to have been much respected. Thus she was able to play a key role in a number of major historical events, the first of which was Attila's siege of Paris in 451.

---

[10] I have described all this in chapter 2 of *Ten Dates Every Catholic Should Know*.

The reputation of the Huns had preceded them, and the Parisians were in a panic. Genevieve advised penance and reliance on God's protection, but many of the terrified citizens favored evacuating the city. Genevieve then addressed the women of Paris, telling them that the men could do as they liked but that she and the other women would remain, praying so hard that God would have to hear them. The men remained, Attila lifted the siege, and Paris was saved. We do not know all his reasons for giving it up, but he was known to have an almost superstitious awe for saintly people, and perhaps what he had heard of Genevieve persuaded him not to do battle with her. The same thing happened in another French city, Troyes, where Bishop Lupus went out to confront the Hun wearing his episcopal robes. Impressed with his courage, Attila spared that city too. (He may have spared too many; certainly he never got his great new empire built.)

We will meet Genevieve again, repelling another would-be occupier of her beloved city, but first we must look at another one of those tribes that Attila had stirred up during his career, and which were now on the move in search of conquests of their own. The tribe was one of a group of peoples known as the Franks, with whom the Romans had long been familiar as a cross-border nuisance. The key issue here, as far as the conversion of the West is concerned, is that virtually all the tribes—including most of the Frankish peoples—were not just menaces to the Roman order. The great danger they posed for the Church and its converts was that they were—with only one major exception—Arians.

How did that happen? Did not Constantine and the Council of Nicaea condemn Arianism and banish its adherents from ecclesiastical office? They did. Those Arians or Arian sympathizers, including the same Bishop Eusebius who allegedly baptized Constantine, advised the Roman Arians as to what they should do next. When a talented young Christian Goth, Ulfilas, was sent by his local church to a council at Antioch in 341, he met the Arian-leaning Eusebius—who made him a bishop. Besides creating perhaps the first barbarian Arian successor of the apostles, Eusebius also seems to have urged him to develop a Gothic alphabet in which the scriptures—with suitably Arian glosses—could be disseminated among the Goths. Ulfilas simplified and tailored this synthetic religion to suit the warrior mentality of his people; it became part of their identity, and it brought with it a hostility to both Roman civilization and Catholicism. As Daniel-Rops cogently explains, the Arian peoples developed a sort of nationalism that was reinforced by their victorious campaigns; Catholicism was to them the religion of the losers.[11] By the time the Salian Franks come into our story, they are the only major pagan tribe left; all the rest of the barbarian groups displaced by the Huns, including the other Frankish tribes, had become Arians. That Gaul had only a pagan invasion to deal with turned out to be a great blessing.

The Women Who Tamed the Barbarians

In 481, the new king of the Salian Franks was a tough 15-year-old named Clovis. As he led his warriors on raids deeper and deeper into Gaul, the Gallo-Roman population prepared for the worst. In Reims, the bishop was not only a saint but a politically and psychologically astute man named Remigius, who, wishing to cultivate an amicable relationship with the young leader, wrote him a letter that would be quoted by the contemporary historian Gregory of Tours. It is a model of diplomacy, avoiding religious issues but addressing topics that might be of interest to a young man so newly come to such a high position. It was a small beginning to what would prove a close relationship of great historical importance.

Meanwhile, the marauding Franks showed no sign of abandoning their violent custom of raiding and pillaging wherever they went. In one case they looted the treasures of a church that included a large and beautiful vase. The bishop of the place

---

[11] Daniel-Rops, *The Church in the Dark Ages*, p. 183.

appealed to Clovis to return that one object, and the king agreed. At the town of Soissons, the army settled down to divide the loot; Clovis, like his soldiers, had the right to a certain percentage of it, but he also announced that in addition he was claiming the vase. One of the soldiers, angered that the king seemed to be taking more than his agreed-upon share, fell into a rage and struck the vase with his battleaxe, breaking it in two. Clovis said nothing, but had the vase mended and returned to the bishop with apologies for its condition. A year later, he was reviewing his troops and, passing along the line, came to the vase-smasher. The king began to criticize everything about his equipment, including the condition of his weapon, which he threw to the ground. As the man stooped to pick it up, Clovis raised his battleaxe and smashed the man's head. "That," he said calmly, "is what you did to the vase of Soissons."

Clovis was a tough and ruthless teenager for sure, and one who could harbor a grudge and punish ruthlessly. His wife Clotilda must have seen other things in him. The biographer of Clotilda, Godefroy Kurth, discussing a letter of St. Jerome on the influence of Christian women, makes an observation that certainly pertains to the period in which Clotilda lived.[12] He says that the secret of the conversion of the Roman world was the tremendous role played by women. Roman wives and mothers who became Christian, often secretly at first, were able to influence their husbands, children, friends, and servants. Their sphere of influence, in fact, was much broader than would appear at first sight. Even Christian slaves had such a sphere, which included their mistresses, fellow slaves, and the tradesmen they dealt with. Those women more highly placed—one thinks of St. Helena—had still more scope, both as role models and patronesses of missionary activity. Yet another class of truly heroic Christian women comprises those who married barbarians in the hope of converting them. Educated, civilized products of Roman culture,

---

[12] Kurth, p. 4.

they burned with the desire to bring all these benefits, through the faith, to the peoples who became theirs by marriage.

Clotilda was raised a Catholic at the court of her Burgundian father, and after his death Clovis asked her family for Clotilda's hand. She was then about 19 and the king was in his 20s. They seem to have been a truly devoted couple, and it was Clotilda's many virtues as well as the friendship of St. Remigius that caused Clovis later to enter the Church. (Some sources say that Genevieve was acquainted with his father and that Clovis as a child may have met her. If so, her influence too may have disposed him to favor Christianity.) When their first child was born, Clovis acquiesced to have the baby baptized. When the child died soon afterward, it must have tried the patience of a man whose pagan friends and Arian sister might well have used the tragedy to discredit the faith and its sacraments. Would not the old gods of the Franks, or the newer Arian god, have protected the heir of the king? So great was his love for Clotilda, however, that he allowed their second child to be baptized. The later illness of that baby must have produced a tense situation; fortunately, the child recovered.

Meanwhile, Clovis was expanding his authority over all the tribes of the Franks and taking over more and more of Gaul. He wished to enter Paris—which was strategically important, though it would only become the Frankish capital under later kings—and apparently expected no difficulty in doing so. He reckoned without Genevieve. She was then about 70 years old and had not only defended the city against Attila but had also rallied the Parisians to withstand a long siege by another barbarian chief. The latter had ended up abandoning the siege and negotiating. She still had about 20 years to live and she was not about to surrender her beloved city to a young pagan, even if his wife was Catholic.

Paris was centered on a large island in the Seine, though it included both banks of the river; when besieged, the population on the banks could simply take refuge in the island fortifications.

When Clovis came huffing and puffing to the shores of the Seine and Genevieve refused him entrance, he was stuck. It had apparently not occurred to him that he might need boats. Genevieve and the Parisians had lots of them, though, and she herself used them to travel the river at night bringing back provisions to the city; there was no possibility of starving the Parisians out, and Clovis had to withdraw. (Later on, during a famine, the indomitable saint repeated her success in provisioning the city, traveling long distances to find food for her people.)

In the year 496 everything changed for Clovis, Clotilda, Genevieve, and France. Clovis was fighting one of his many battles and getting the worst of it. The thought occurred to him to pray to Clotilda's God, since whomever his pagan gods were, they were clearly of no use at that moment. He did pray, apparently promising to become a Christian, as Clotilda had often urged him, if his army was successful. He won the battle, which caused him to do some serious thinking about religion. He made a pilgrimage to St. Martin's shrine at Tours. (Clotilda had already been there seeking the saint's aid in converting her husband, and Genevieve had come pleading for help for her city; from heaven, Martin still had a lot of work to do.) Clovis now asked St. Martin for the grace of being able to persuade his soldiers to join him in the faith.

The king of the Franks was instructed in the faith by St. Remigius and then baptized and anointed with holy chrism. Accounts of the ceremony tell how the king stopped at the door of Remigius's church (on the site of the present Reims Cathedral), overawed by the brilliant lights, music, and singing. "Father, is this the heaven you promised me?" "No, my son, but it is the beginning of the road that leads there." Many of his soldiers followed him into the Church, and the conversion of their king had a beneficial influence on the whole Frankish population. The example given by their king inspired imitation by his people, as other tribes had adopted the Arianism of their chiefs. Thus, only 20 years after the date often used for the fall of Rome—476, when a Gothic chief deposed the last emperor—there was, amid a sea of Arianism, a strong Catholic king in Gaul. The year 496 is a light in the gathering darkness of a period called the Dark Ages that opened soon—too soon—following the felicitous reign of Clovis and Clotilda.

As for Genevieve, she now welcomed the Catholic king and his wife into Paris and became a great friend and counselor of the royal family. By this time she had become an influential member of the municipal council of Paris, so great was her reputation. Even from Clovis's pagan father she had extracted favors, such as the freeing of prisoners and clemency for criminals, and Clovis continued to grant her requests.[13] Clotilda, after her husband's death in 511, retired for a time to the monastery of St. Martin in Tours, which reminds us yet again of Martin's reputation for hearing and granting the prayers of his suppliants.

The Darkness Falls, and Small Lights Emerge

To Clotilda's great distress, the sons of Clovis turned out to be incompetent, almost vicious characters who were incapable of providing the Franks with good government. Their mother's long widowhood was filled with suffering at the crimes and quarrels of the family she had tried to imbue with Christian principles. Often she found herself on the road, trying to heal some family breach or other, or consoling some bereaved or abandoned wife. As a saint, she is certainly a model of motherly heroism. So incompetent were the later descendents of Clovis in what is known as the Merovingian dynasty that they were called "the do-nothing kings." Degenerate and frivolous, they wiled away their time in their palaces or at trivial pastimes, leaving the actual business of running the Frankish kingdom to officials known as mayors of the palace.

This period, from the middle of the sixth to the early eighth century, is known as the Dark Ages. Not all the lights went out,

---

13 Mondot, p. 106.

of course—the monasteries still existed and there was still a pope in Rome—but what was left of classical civilization stagnated, then declined, and gradually passed out of memory. The Gothic rulers of Rome were not totally illiterate or incompetent, but they lacked the Roman genius for government as well as the skills that had kept the aqueducts, buildings, and roads of the empire in good repair. Roman schools and libraries were allowed to decay and collapse. The tribes that occupied the bits and pieces of the former empire beyond Italy were not inclined to rebuild what they had demolished in battle, so cities declined into towns, and then into villages—when they survived at all. Peasants turned for their work and protection to their landlords, as they had begun to do in the days of Diocletian. In return, they agreed not to leave the land; free farmers became serfs, the human building blocks of feudalism.

The Church? It was the last stronghold of literacy and learning, as bishops took over the tasks done by Roman administrators and educators. For a time, until the decay became overwhelming, city life was often kept going by the administrative skills of bishops. They organized defenses (like the bishop we saw defending his people against the Huns) and tried to keep up what they could of civilized life. Ignorance and lack of spiritual formation took their toll on the clergy as well. When those who should have taught the people were themselves either ignorant or corrupt, one can only imagine the spiritual and moral condition of the faithful.

The only bright lights in this growing darkness were the monasteries, mainly offshoots of those founded by St. Benedict in the early sixth century. It often happens that what saints think they should do with their lives turns out not to be what God wants done with them. Benedict came from a noble Roman family in Italy. He seems to have had a good education and enjoyed life in society until he was about 20 years old, around the year 500, when he decided to get away from the social whirl for a time. He did not intend to become a hermit, but when he met a holy man named Romanus in the mountains, he retired to a cave for a time. Eventually, he discovered his true vocation, which was to form a society of men who would live according to his Rule, a work of genius and divine guidance.

So popular did this first little community become that it soon had too many aspirants for one monastery and had to expand. In Benedict's lifetime, 12 small communities were founded, dedicated to his ideals of prayer, work, and study, and also providing small schools for children. By the time of our do-nothing kings in the Frankish kingdom, Benedictine houses had spread throughout much of the former Roman Empire and were providing an invaluable service unforeseen by their founder: preserving books. Except for a handful of original Roman manuscripts, everything that we have today of classical texts comes from monastery libraries, where monks laboriously copied every manuscript, both spiritual and secular, they could collect. Centuries would pass until readers would again be taught to understand and study those books. Meanwhile, back to the mayors of the palace in the land of the Franks.

Restoring Christian Kingship

While the mayors of the palace were trying to hold their realm together, with no cooperation from those who wore the kingly crowns, an ominous development was taking place far from Europe that would affect its destiny. Just as the existence of the Huns was unknown to the peoples of the West until Huns suddenly appeared out of the East, so did the next wave of invasion catch most kingdoms unprepared. Of the three waves of assault that broke over the dying Roman Empire, we have already seen the first: the barbarians and Huns in the 400s and 500s. We now come to the second: the warriors of Islam.

These invaders came roiling out of Arabia, galvanized by a new militant religion as well as by a desire for loot. They swept north into the Eastern Empire and west across North Africa; from Africa they raided the Mediterranean coasts of Europe, at one point getting as far as the gates of Rome. When they crossed into Spain with numerous North African Berber allies in 711, it was not merely to raid and run; they took almost the entire peninsula from the ruling Arian Visigoths, with the exception of a small pocket of Christian resistance, and they were there to stay. That resistance, however, would grow and become the great *Reconquista* that would take back Spain for the Spaniards—but not for a long time.

Meanwhile, an energetic and extremely competent family had emerged to occupy the office of mayor of the palace in Merovingian France. At the time of the Moorish invasion, the mayor was one Charles Martel—Charles the Hammer—a talented general and commanding leader. The Moors in Spain now looked northward for new conquests, or at least new sources of spoils, and in 732 they headed across the French border for St. Martin's old city of Tours, with its shrines and treasures. Charles went to meet them. Though the subsequent battle is variously called the Battle of Tours or the Battle of Poitiers, it occurred somewhere between the two cities. It was a hard-fought, all-day battle, but Martel's army succeeded in repelling the enemy, which melted back into Spain. This significant victory did not end Muslim forays into southern France nor put a stop to the raids on the coasts, but it likely prevented a full-scale invasion. Moreover, it enhanced the reputation of the mayor of the palace.

Charles's successor, his son Pepin, took the bold step of consulting the pope as to who, in the opinion of the sovereign pontiff, should have the title and authority of king in France: the man who had the name of king or the one who actually did the job of governing and defending the realm? The Church in France had been suffering from a number of ills since the demise of Clovis and Clotilda. Those sovereigns had not only built churches and monasteries but had supported the work of the Church in all areas and had encouraged sound religious orders and a capable clergy. With little help or direction from the "do-nothing kings," the Frankish church developed so many problems that a synod

was held in 742—presided over by St. Boniface, the great apostle
of Germany—to sort things out. Pepin's question to Pope Zach-
arias thus affected church and state alike, and so did the pope's
answer. The one who did the job of governing, he said, should
hold the title and authority. Whereupon the last idle Merovingian was deposed and Pepin was consecrated king of the Franks.

Thus began a fruitful and long-lasting alliance between the
kingdom of the Franks and the papacy. It was Pepin who established the Papal States, a sorely needed buffer zone for papal
Rome against the various marauders that periodically infested
Italy. The independence of the papacy would have been greatly
compromised had it fallen under the control of those invaders; Pepin and then his son, the great Charlemagne, guaranteed
that independence. Both rulers also cooperated closely with the
Church in the Frankish kingdom in the work of converting
the remaining pagans and promoting sound teaching, an educated clergy, and the spread of monasteries. It was Charlemagne,
Charles the Great, who promoted all this with the greatest energy.

Charlemagne and Conversion

Through conquest of some of the neighboring regions (he
fought 60 major campaigns in 30 years) and the voluntary submission of others, in time Charles ruled a far larger empire than
Clovis had dreamed of. He was king not only of the Frankish kingdom of France but of a vast territory that included the
Frankish areas that are now Germany, parts of eastern Europe
(Croatia, Bohemia, Moravia), and some of northern Italy; except
for Spain, he ruled more or less the whole of Europe. His capital was not Paris, too far to the west, but Aachen, closer to the
middle of his realm.

Much could be said of how admirably he administered this
sprawling empire, fostering a sense of unity among the disparate
peoples while still allowing them their own laws and customs,
and how concerned he was for justice. What interests us here is
his zeal for the care of the Church. In addition to the financial

support he gave to monasteries and church-building projects, he promoted reform everywhere.

The clergy of the Dark Ages was often poorly educated, sometimes worldly, and even morally corrupt. Certainly there were many pious and zealous priests, but learning was far more likely to be found in monasteries than at the parish level. When Charlemagne came to power, examples began to turn up of priests so ignorant of Latin that they garbled the words used in the administration of the sacraments. This was shocking, and the emperor was also shocked by the borderline-illiterate writing in letters he received from monks, containing "both correct thoughts and uncouth expressions; because what pious devotion dictated faithfully to the mind, the tongue, uneducated on account of the neglect of study, was not able to express in the letters without error."[14] He therefore decided to use the monasteries as schools for the clergy, in which they would learn not only sound doctrine but also the language tools they needed.

Education was a prime concern for Charlemagne, who could read and who spoke a number of languages, though he never got the hang of writing. He brought scholars to Aachen wherever he could find them; his head schoolmaster and librarian was the English scholar Alcuin, for example. At court, he set up a prototype school for both boys and girls, taking classes himself in subjects he did not know. Then he ordered schools for children to be set up all over the empire. For the first time since the fall of Rome, a thoroughgoing revival of learning was begun: It is called, after Charles, "the Carolingian Renaissance."

It was too brief. Following the death of Charlemagne's son, who succeeded him briefly, the empire was divided into what would later become modern France, Germany, and a "middle kingdom" in between them. So far so good, but that third wave of invaders now struck from two directions: Vikings poured out of Scandinavia, and another mass of warriors from Asia,

---

[14] Perry, p. 208.

the Magyars, raced into Europe from the east. We will see in a later chapter how these violent pagan horsemen became a great Christian nation.

The Year 1000: A Balance Sheet

The 900s were a grim time in which to live, as the next two chapters will show. The pagan sea raiders from Scandinavia poured up and down the rivers of Europe, sailing into Paris by way of the Seine, and reaching what would later become Ukraine by sailing down the river systems from the Baltic. They took over Mediterranean islands, besieged Byzantium, settled Iceland, and probably reached North America. The northern part of England they occupied, and everywhere they looted what they could use and destroyed what they could not—such as the precious books in the monastic libraries of Ireland and England. Some communities on the western coasts of Europe fled inland in fear of the marauders, only to meet—and be massacred by—those savage nomads moving in from the east. It was no good moving south, for the Saracens were still raiding the southern coasts and in some places gaining footholds. Central political authority had disappeared or was neutralized in most of the continent, and country people depended increasingly on local warriors to defend them; the warriors, in turn, depended on the farmers—the serfs—for food and help with their animals and domestic work. By the end of the 10th century, there were no true cities left on the continent of Europe, and fewer than 12 towns of any size. Most of the schools had disappeared, like the monasteries, except for those monasteries that had become the property of local warlords.

No wonder some people thought it was a fitting time for the world to end, with so much gone already. As Chesterton put it in *The Ballad of the White Horse,* describing the sentiments of someone living through that time:

> For the end of the world was long ago—
> And all we dwell today

As children of some second birth,
Like a strange people left on earth
After a judgment day.

When Caesar's sun fell out of the sky
And whoso harkened right
Could only hear the plunging
Of the nations in the night."

Yet the end did not come.

Incredibly, by the 11th century, on this side of the year 1000,
a number of good things had happened. The raids had ceased;
the marauders had settled down. The ruler of the Magyars was
a Catholic saint and had received an apostolic crown from the
pope. The Vikings were busy demonstrating the unlikely talent
of urban construction: They began to build cities in the areas
they had previously ravaged. Almost unnoticed, back in the year
910, a generous nobleman in France hatched the idea of endowing a monastery that would answer only to the pope, with complete independence from local political authority. By the new
millennium the idea had expanded to other areas and was poised
to begin a great reform movement within the Church.

In short, as the Benedictine chronicler Raoul Glaber wrote of
this happy time, "It seemed as if the world, shaking itself and cast-
ing off its old age, was putting on, here, there, and everywhere,
the pure white garment of churches." Building, cultivation of
the land, the revival of town life and commerce—all these were
beginning to appear again. What was most needed, however, was
the evangelization of those hoards of pagan invaders; that was the
daunting task—among other daunting tasks, true—of the 10th
and 11th centuries, as will soon be seen.

It is marvelous to note that the West was able to take up these
tasks after the upheavals and destruction it had suffered since
the fall of Rome. Waves of barbarian invasions, massive physical
destruction, illiteracy, and ignorance had plagued the continent

for centuries. The dawn of a new Christian civilization was hampered by the slow pace of conversion, the persistence of pagan religions and heresies such as Arianism, and especially by the arrival of new masses of pagans, who not only destroyed the earlier efforts (often by destroying the missionaries) but also brought their own alien religions and alien ways of thinking. The conversion of large chunks of the former Roman Empire had, in short, to be begun anew; so did that of areas that had never been part of the empire, such as Scandinavia and Eastern Europe.

In this new age, Catholic France would play a major role. Whether in Church reform, education, or missionary work, the seeds planted by the great missionaries we have met in this chapter would produce spectacular fruit.

In the providential conversion of Clovis and the Salian Franks, in the fidelity and courage of Martin, Genevieve, and Clotilda, we find one of the lynchpins of Christian history. Had the kingdom of France, and Charlemagne's larger empire, not been converted to Catholicism, if Arianism had become the state religion of those areas, or if paganism had continued to hold sway in their wide rural regions, we would record a vastly different history. We can speculate on a few examples of how the Arians behaved when they had political power. The Arian Vandals in North Africa, who were a pretty violent and unpleasant people, tried to force their heresy down the throats of their subjects, banishing orthodox clergy and closing monasteries. Among the Germanic tribes, on the other hand, the Arian upper classes do not seem to have interfered much with their Catholic subjects. What was more common was the poisoning of the mental and spiritual atmosphere. Not only did Arians deny the divinity of Christ; they had no taste for Christian learning. The writings of the Fathers and Doctors of the Church, and even of the classical Roman writers, held no interest for them. Indeed, they seem to have had an antipathy to Roman culture because of its association with

Roman Christianity and also because they wanted to preserve their barbarian heritage, which had come to be so closely bound up with their heresy. They were thus a roadblock not only to the orthodox faith but also to the transmission of civilization through the Dark Ages.

Their days, however, even in the areas they still held around the year 1000, were numbered. The most spectacular flourishing of civilization in history was to be Catholic, not Arian, and as dedicated to the conversion of the nations as were the Catholics whose world we have glimpsed in this chapter.

෨ INSTRUMENTS OF CONVERSION ෬

MONASTERIES

From early Christian times there had been hermits in the Egyptian desert and elsewhere, and then small communities of men and women who wanted to leave the world and devote themselves to prayer and penance. By the sixth century, St. Benedict of Nursia would be organizing monks and nuns into somewhat different and highly successful communities of prayer, work, and study according to his Rule. Although these communities were ordered, like all monasteries, to the sanctification of their members, they would have incalculable and unforeseen benefits for the emerging Christian civilization. Throughout the Dark Ages, monks and nuns will be the teachers, nurses, artists, missionaries, spiritual directors, medical advisers, and instructors in agricultural science of whom barbarian Europe was so greatly in need. In this time we also come across pre-Benedictine communities of monks who are also missionaries, a preview of future preaching and teaching orders.

One invaluable contribution of the Dark Age monasteries not only provided essential tools for evangelization but enriched Western civilization immeasurably: this was the copying of books. The monks of the period copied prayer books, Bibles, doctrinal treatises; they also transmitted to the modern world virtually all the classical literature we possess. They even copied scientific and other classical works that were beyond their comprehension in the hope that someday men more learned than they would be able to make use of them. That is exactly what happened when the medieval renaissance of learning began to unfold centuries later. It was primarily the preservation of the irreplaceable works of the Fathers and Doctors of the Church, however, in addition to Scripture, that made the copying of countless monks over the centuries a powerful instrument for maintaining and spreading the faith.

England and Ireland: the First Millenium

Iona

PICTS

5th century

Ireland

St. Patrick
5th century

Danes invade,
9th century

663 Synod of Whitby

5th century

SAXONS

Alfred the Great
unifies England
9th century

Angles
5th Century

London

Vessex

Canterbury

St. Augustine
arrives 597

3

The Sceptered Isle and the Emerald Isle

To the far northwest of Rome, up there in the fog across the water from Gaul, the Roman Empire came to an end on the island of Britain. The legions had never made it all the way to its northernmost tip because of the mountainous terrain with its fierce inhabitants, and they had not attempted the conquest of Ireland at all. Missionaries, however, were active on both islands; their successes helped shape all Christian history, and that is the theme of this chapter.

The conversion of Britain should be a straightforward topic, but it turns out to be anything but. The earliest sources are sketchy, and many theories propounded about early British Christianity conceal a religious or political agenda. Some claim that there was no Christianity on the island until the Anglo-Saxon invasions of the Dark Ages—just that charming and superior Druid religion that was so wrongly suppressed later on. Others claim that the British received Christianity as early as the first century and that the British Celtic church developed its own distinctive doctrines and practices suited to the mentality of its members and superior to those of what was to become the corrupt Church of Rome. When the Roman representatives of the papistical continental Church came to Britain, they largely succeeded in suppressing that nice British Church. This, the story goes, was one of those Bad Things of history, a wrong that was not to be righted until the glorious Reformation.

If we look only at the facts, insofar as these are known at all, we can conclude that there *was* a very early presence of Christians in Roman Britain. This is not surprising, since the island was first visited by Julius Caesar during the days of the Republic and then later incorporated into the empire. We have some Roman descriptions of the Celtic people they called Britons. Julius

Caesar, who invaded Britain twice and liked to write chatty accounts of all the places he visited, described the residents of Kent as being civilized to some degree, something like the Gauls, but generally barbarians with odd customs, multiple wives, and a Druid religion. After the island became part of the empire there would have been soldiers, administrators, and businessmen, as well as numerous slaves, stationed there during the early Christian period. There is an elusive claim in some early sources that it was St. Paul (some say Joseph of Arimathea) who first brought the faith to the island; this reminds us of the stories of the New Testament saints who supposedly went to Apt in Gaul, though it rests on less evidence than those.

According to St. Bede, in his famous *History of the English Church and People*, it was in the year 156 that, "while the holy Eleutherus ruled the Roman Church, Lucius, a British king, sent him a letter, asking to be made a Christian by his direction. This pious request was quickly granted, and the Britons received the faith and held it peacefully in all its purity and fullness until the time of the Emperor Diocletian."[15] This is a good straightforward statement that one would like to accept; unfortunately, it does not seem to find general acceptance among historians. Little is known about St. Eleutherus and nothing for certain about his dealings with King Lucius (if there was a King Lucius).

We *seem* to be on somewhat more solid ground by the time of Diocletian's persecution of 303, because we hear of three British martyrs, among whom St. Alban is the best known. According to Bede and other sources of the period, he was a pagan who gave shelter to a priest during the persecution and became a Christian and a martyr himself, praying for his murderers as he died. Even here, however, things are not so clear. Diocletian and his co-emperor, Galerius, certainly did launch the worst of the persecutions. Britain was then under the rule of Constantius, father of Constantine, who seems to have been reluctant to engage in

---

15 Bede, p. 42.

persecution and certainly did not enforce anti-Christian measures later on. Did he do so in 303? We do not know. It has therefore been proposed that the British martyrs were actually killed in persecutions of the previous century. This makes more historical sense, and some early sources do mention the earlier Emperor Severus. As was the case in France, however, from the blood of the early British martyrs (in whatever year they died) would come a great harvest.

At any rate, it is certain that Christianity was established in Britain by at least the third century. In the fourth century, there is mention in various chronicles of British bishops at several Church councils of the time; there were three of them at the Council of Arles in 314, and others are mentioned at Nicaea in 325. We recall that Constantine's Edict of Milan had been issued in 313, and that during the fourth century the whole empire gradually became at least nominally Christian. This was the case in Britain too, though the actual number of practicing Christian Britons at that time was said to be few; there were also occasional flickers of a resurgent paganism evidenced by the building of new temples. Certainly the country was Christian enough, ironically, to become a hotbed of Pelagianism, one of the worst heresies to dog the early Church. Any heresy produces resistance to conversion, of course, but one that preaches an easier way to heaven than does the Church must prove an especially formidable obstacle for Catholic missionaries, and so it was with the seductive errors of Pelagius.

Pelagius and His Novel Doctrine

The essence of what has become known as Pelagianism, named for its founder, Pelagius, is a denial of original sin, from which further false concepts logically follow. Among these are the notions that Adam would have died even if he had not sinned—since there is no connection between sin and death—and that, since children are born sinless, there is no need for infant baptism. As for how one should live in order to get to heaven, Pelagius seems to have claimed that the Law of Moses was as good a guide as the Gospels.

All these propositions were condemned by Rome in 418, and the Emperor Honorius went so far as to ban Pelagians from Italy. But from the time that Pelagius and his colleague in heresy, Caelestius, burst onto the theological scene in the early fifth century, they had at least 10 years before their condemnation in which to acquire disciples for their false teaching. Scholars such as St. Jerome recognized their doctrines as erroneous, and St. Augustine soon became the great champion of orthodoxy against the heresy. That it took so long for it to be identified and condemned was partly because of the slipperiness of some of the wording used by the heretics and partly because the popes, first Pope Innocent I and then Pope Zosimus, were ill informed as to what Pelagius and company were teaching. (Upheavals such as the sack of Rome by the Visigoths in 410 made communication that much more difficult.)

In the end, both Caelestius and Pelagius seem to have submitted to the Church, but the fact that the Council of Ephesus had to condemn Pelagianism again in 431 shows how tenacious were their ideas. In fact, the Church was still dealing with them and issuing condemnations into the next century. As for Roman Britain, it comes into the Pelagian story in two ways. First, Pelagius was often said in his own time to have come from Britain; St. Jerome referred to him rather vaguely as being "of the Scots people, from the area of the Britons," and added a disparaging remark about him being "a porridge-eater." Some recent scholars, on the other hand, argue that "Scots" here really indicates that Pelagius was from Ireland. The consensus of his contemporaries, though, seems to have been that he was—as his nickname *Britannicus* shows—a Briton. Certainly his heresy took stubborn root in Britain, after infecting Gaul, and those two areas became its centers. We find missionaries like St. Germanus and St. Lupus of Troyes battling the virus first in Gaul and then crossing the Channel to fight it again in Britain. When they had succeeded in silencing the British defenders of the heresy, they credited St. Alban, proto-martyr of England. They carefully opened his tomb and added to it relics of some apostles and martyrs that they had brought to St. Alban as a token of their gratitude.[16]

In the 500s, the heresy seems to have turned up briefly in Wales, after which it disappears.[17] (Some later Protestant teachings seem to echo at least a few of Pelagius's tenets, and some of them still seem to be around today.) Although the heresy did not spread as far or penetrate the temporal powers as deeply as Arianism had, it still took its toll—which, for the early British Church, was doctrinal confusion. Perhaps this weakened orthodox British Christianity in the trial that was soon to come; certainly St. Bede, in his famous history of the Church in England, lays blame on the British Christians for not doing more to convert the next wave of invaders of the island, though he may have exaggerated their inertia.

The End of Roman Britain

We saw in the previous chapter how the pressure of the Huns' migration westward pushed other tribes into the Roman Empire, where in many cases they settled down and could not be dislodged. Something similar happened to Britain at the same time, that is, the late fourth and fifth centuries. The island had been no stranger to barbaric invasion even before the arrival of the Germanic tribes. Periodically, the Picts from Scotland descended upon the Britons from the north. Their name may be of Latin origin, since the Romans had grim experience of these fierce, hairy fighters who either tattooed or painted their bodies (hence Picts: "painted people" or "pictured ones"). It was largely to keep them at bay that the Emperor Hadrian had built his famous wall across the island. Emperor Antoninus Pius later added another wall, further north, but the Romans were forced

---

[16] Guéranger, vol. 3, p. 236.
[17] Pohle, "Pelagius."

to abandon it and pull back to Hadrian's Wall. (We find later Britons trying to find safety from barbarian attacks "between the two walls.")

Under the onslaught of invasions from so many directions and unable to maintain all their far-flung borders intact, the Romans began to withdraw from the further reaches of their empire; their departure left the Romanized civilian populations at the mercy of often ruthless marauders. As early as 408, following a raid by the Germanic Saxons, who had begun entrenching themselves on the British coast, Emperor Honorius had decreed that the Britons had to organize their own defense. One can imagine the sinking feeling that must have overwhelmed the citizens of coastal British towns as they watched the last Roman ships sail out of sight. In the later fifth century, the Picts began to raid again and so did the Irish—sometimes confusingly called Scots in the sources. (They may actually have settled in what is now Scotland and thus become the original Scots; did I mention it was confusing?) At one point all three groups, Scots, Picts (who were now cooperating with each other), and Irish raiders, staged a massive and destructive attack on Britain, causing great physical and economic damage and taking many lives. Roman reinforcements had arrived in previous such emergencies, so once again the embattled Britons sent a moving and desperate plea to Rome for help: "The barbarians drive us to the sea, the sea drives us to the barbarians, and so we have a choice of miseries and are either murdered or drowned."[18]

The year, however, was 446, and the city of Rome itself was only a short time away from its own conquest by barbarians; no help came. There were the Saxons, and the Britons in their desperation were driven to beg these new Germanic arrivals for help against the Celtic invaders. It was help they were glad to give, since they had earmarked for Saxon occupation the very places the Celts were attacking. The Celtic marauders were repelled,

---

[18] Duckett, *The Gateway to the Middle Ages*, p. 104.

but again at the cost of great damage and loss of life. Then it was the turn of the Germans to add to the misery of Britain.

Two Germanic tribes, the Angles as well as the Saxons, along with a tribe called Jutes, from the southern part of what is now Denmark, had begun to invade the island in the first years of the fifth century. In many areas resistance was efficiently organized and the civilized populations were able to hold off the barbarians—at least for a while—though, as we have seen, some of them settled in parts of the west coast from which the Britons were unable to dislodge them. By the end of the century, the Saxons were clearly a major menace to the existence of a Britain that was Roman in culture and Christian in religion, even though the Roman Empire no longer governed or defended it. The murderous campaigns of the pagan and barbaric Saxons against the Britons decimated the island until the early sixth century, when the epic Battle of Badon Hill took place, an unexpected and resounding British victory that won for the country a period of much-needed peace. Despite its mention in a number of chronicles, one of them almost contemporary, little is known for sure about this great battle: Its date, location, and the names of the victorious warriors are all uncertain. Intriguingly, some accounts name "Arthur" as the victorious British general—said to be such a great warrior that he was actually able to lead a large British army across the Channel to Gaul and defeat a fleeing force of barbarians there. He became known as the *Restitutor*, the Restorer: of civic order, of peace, of Roman civilization and culture, of Christianity. Legend it may be, or there may be a tantalizing reality behind all the tales and myths.

In time, as happened more than once in the Dark Ages, the barbarian invaders stopped devastating the land and began to settle down to stay more or less peacefully in it, multiplying and building; thus a new Anglo-Saxon England gradually replaced Roman Britain. The crucial question was whether these pagans would adopt Christianity and, through it, civilization itself. As we noted above, Bede reproaches the Britons for not attempting to convert their oppressors. Still, some missionary work must have been done, for when clergy were later sent from Rome they found that at least some of the Anglo-Saxons were already familiar with Christianity. The famous story of how Rome became involved in this conversion story is delightful to come upon, after all the otherwise depressing news from the Dark Ages.

A Tale of Three Saints

St. Gregory the Great came to the papal throne in 590, one of a line of extraordinarily holy popes, most of them canonized. His achievements are too many even to summarize here, and his spiritual writings still make good reading today. He promoted monasticism everywhere, with excellent results, and he was zealous for conversion. He knew of the devastation that the Saxons had brought to Britain and to the Church there and had hoped to undertake a missionary expedition to that people. Once he became pope, he was unable to fulfill his dream in person—there was far too much to attend to in Rome during the grim sixth century—but he was to be the instrument of a great historical development. The story goes that in Rome he once saw some young boys, possibly slaves, with fair skin and hair, and wanted to know who they were. When told they were Angles from Briton, Gregory replied, "No, not Angles but angels."

Perhaps this encounter recalled to him the needs of so many pagan souls in Britain; in any case he sent the future St. Augustine of Canterbury and a few companions to Britain in 596. After one false start and return to Rome, they reached the kingdom of Kent early in 597. There Augustine found our third saint, Ethelbert, at the time King Ethelbert and still a pagan. Like Clovis, he had married a Christian woman named Bertha who had in fact come from Gaul; she was a Frankish princess of the ruling family in Paris, and thus may have been a descendent of St. Clotilda. She brought her chaplain to England with her, and no doubt had prepared her husband for his meeting with the missionary from Rome. He courteously assisted Augustine in his work and gave him every opportunity to travel and preach in Kent.

Although he did not become an instant Christian, Ethelbert's conversion was not long in coming—he was baptized in June 597, the same year Augustine arrived. Thousands of his subjects were said to have followed their king's example. The king ordered the construction of the church that would later become Canterbury Cathedral, the seat of the Primate of England, and helped Augustine turn a pagan temple into a church. He did not, however, force Christianity upon his subjects, or even his children: The two daughters of Ethelbert and Bertha became Catholic, but their only son remained pagan. This must have been a cross for the devout parents, and one with which many modern parents can sympathize. Ethelbert's Catholic nephew Sabert, however, who was king of the East Saxons, assisted the missionary efforts of St. Mellitus (whoops, a fourth saint in this story!), who arrived with the second group of missionaries sent by Gregory in 601, and whom Sabert supported in making London his see.

After Sabert's death, things turned sour. His own sons were not only pagan but also hostile to Mellitus and what he stood for. Once they demanded that he give them "the white bread" that he had given their father, and when he replied that they would have to be baptized first, they banished him from the kingdom. He went to Kent, but was unable to stay there either (perhaps because of that pagan son of Ethelbert), and finally had to withdraw to Gaul. He was able to return to Kent a year later but never managed to get back to his own see of London. All this time he suffered from ill health, and although he worked many miracles, they do not seem to have made him universally popular as St. Martin of Tours's miracles did for him.

Reconciling the Old and the New

It must not be forgotten that the Christian churches and monastic communities that existed in Britain before the coming of Augustine were used to religious customs and practices dating back centuries. Some of those practices were no longer in use in Rome and others had suffered corruption over the centuries from the ignorance of uneducated clergy and lack of knowledge of what correct practice was in the first place. We recall that Charlemagne had to cope with this sort of problem in his day. It was thus necessary for clergy and monks in Britain to fill the gaps in their knowledge, and for this purpose Augustine and other missionaries brought books and documents with them from Rome. Augustine himself met with resistance on the part of a number of British bishops who did not wish to accept his authority on questions of practice. Many areas of the country had been evangelized by Irish monks from the monastery of Iona (whom we will meet later in this chapter), who followed their own ancient practices and calendars. Thus Britain in the seventh century found itself religiously split: Except for a few remaining pockets of paganism it was Catholic in name but divided, often bitterly so, between those who accepted the authority of Rome in practice as well as in doctrine and those who wanted to stick to the old English ways of doing things liturgical.

The main sticking point was the computation of the date on which Easter was to fall each year. At first sight, this seems an odd detail for two parts of the British Church to quarrel over, but it was really very important. Easter is the center, the overwhelmingly important event of the Church year, and upon it the whole rest of the ecclesiastical year depends. If you get the date of Easter wrong, your Septuagesima and Lent will come at the wrong times and so will Pentecost, the Time after Pentecost, and Advent. In a truly Christian society the liturgical year colors the whole culture; customs, special foods, music, etc., develop around the Church seasons and holy days. Since Easter is a movable feast geared to the solar cycle, it comes on a different date every year. From the earliest Christian times there had been various ways of determining the date, and the Council of Nicaea finally decreed that the feast should be on the Sunday following the first full moon after the vernal equinox, as it still is today.

The Church in Britain, having received the faith prior to the council and having been largely cut off from contact with Rome, was used to figuring out Easter in its own way. The unwillingness of some members of that Church to accept the decision of Nicaea, once it had been made known to them, may have simply sprung from a dislike of any change in the way they had always lived the liturgical year. For others, resistance may have signified an unwillingness to accept the authority of Rome. In 663, the question was resolved at the Synod of Whitby. The representatives of Rome were supported by a bishop of Paris who had held office in Britain and knew the mentality there, and the local king used his influence in favor of the Roman usage. Most of the clergy submitted to the synod, though some diehard Irish monks on the island of Iona held out until 716 before accepting "the Roman Easter."[19]

A British Christian Identity Is Forged

Finally unified under Roman authority, the Church in Britain could organize and expand throughout the country. In addition to the establishment of bishoprics, another important development occurred: the setting up of parishes within dioceses, according to the system first created in Gaul by Martin of Tours. The seventh and eighth centuries were thus a time of growth but also of trials. The year following the Synod of Whitby, both Britain and Ireland were struck by the deadly Yellow Plague, perhaps a form of jaundice, which had already ravaged the continent of Europe. Bede describes its arrival: "In the same year of our Lord 664...a sudden plague, which first decimated the southern parts of Britain and later spread into the province of the Northumbrians, raged for a long time and brought widespread death to many people....The plague was equally destructive in Ireland."[20] There were also power struggles among the several kings who

---

[19] Whitelock, pp. 160-161.
[20] Bede, p. 195.

ruled the kingdoms of Britain. Occasionally we see elusive references in contemporary documents to someone who seems to have been a super-king, with exceptional military prowess and prestige, but in fact the political unification of the island would have a long time to wait. Monasteries there had been from the early period of Christian Britain, and in the absence of new invasions and the presence of local political order, these were able to flourish and grow throughout the seventh and eighth centuries.

Then came the ninth century, and with it the Danes. These fierce Vikings—part of the last great wave of invasion to hit Europe after the fall of Rome—had already struck Ireland in the late eighth century, and now they turned their attention to England, defeating one kingdom after the other, murdering and pillaging. This devastation produced a curious effect. According to one historian, the Vikings "constituted the common enemy, making the English the more conscious of a national identity which overrode deeper distinctions; they could be perceived as an instrument of divine punishment for the people's sins, raising awareness of a collective Christian identity; and by 'conquering' the kingdoms of the East Angles, the Northumbrians, and the Mercians they created a vacuum in the leadership of the English people which was waiting to be filled."[21]

The times produced the man: a national hero, a unifier of the English people, and a great Catholic scholar.

King Alfred the Great

Alfred inherited the throne of Wessex in 871, when he was about 20 years old, and ruled until his death in 899. Most of his reign was spent leading armies against the fierce incursions of the Danes and liberating areas they already held, such as the city of London. The period was a time of calamities for much of the West, not just England. The Saracens were still attacking

---

[21] Keynes, "England 700-900," in *The New Cambridge Medieval History*, vol. II, p. 41.

the shores of Italy in force and even threatening Rome. Viking devastations in the lands ruled by Charlemagne's successors were widespread as the seafarers sailed down the rivers and along the coasts, burning, looting, and enslaving prisoners. These invaders were not interested merely in loot, as the Scandinavians who had come in earlier centuries had been; they wanted to settle down permanently in areas they found attractive. Thus they conquered and settled Normandy on the coast of France, and much of the island of Britain.

Even Alfred was unable to expel them completely from the Anglo-Saxon territories he controlled, and he was sometimes forced to buy off the invaders or make truces with them. As a teenager he had fought them by the side of his older brother, then king of Wessex, and when he succeeded to the throne his military career continued off and on until his death. The year following his accession was a low point in the struggle: the Danes had succeeded in taking over virtually all of the country except for Wessex. Alfred changed that situation dramatically. He had the vision to realize that the beleaguered Anglo-Saxons needed a larger and better fleet if they were going to fight seamen; he had one built and with it won a number of sea battles. He also won some spectacular victories against the Danes on land, along with the allegiance of the entire Anglo-Saxon people.

Alfred's government was known for its justice, and the king himself drew up a new law code, "based on the Ten Commandments given by God to Moses, fulfilled and interpreted by the love and compassion of his Son, the Healer, the Lord Christ, continued in the teachings of the Apostles, and thence down the ages by synods of the Church and decrees of kings."[22] He issued decrees against sorcery and witchcraft and promoted the administration of justice and good government at the local level. As if all this were not enough, we must mention, though briefly, Alfred's promotion of education and learning and his own literary efforts.

---

[22] Duckett, *Alfred the Great*, p. 91.

His people had become more ignorant and uneducated than their ancestors because of the absence of teachers and the destruction of schools and libraries by their enemies. Alfred himself had not been well educated as a child, and as king he tried to make up for it by studying. (One wonders where he found the time!) He even persevered in studying Latin and making laborious translations, producing his own version of St. Augustine's *Soliloquies* that he called *Flowers*. He was, in short, like Charlemagne in his zeal for the faith, for good government, for the defense of his people, and for learning. He died October 26, 899, not quite 50 years old.

As for his country, it had come a long way since its pagan days and was on its way to becoming, in the next century, a civilized Catholic kingdom that would produce literary masterpieces, political institutions, saints, and great missionaries—some of whom we will meet in their missions on the continent. There remained, perhaps, that latent tendency to consider the "English way" of doing things as superior to that of the Latins—even if one of those Latins was the pope. The same religious nationalism can be found to some degree in other countries, but in England it would have the most tragic results.

The Isle of Saints and Scholars

Ireland, which unlike Britain had never been ruled by the Romans, received the faith somewhat earlier than the Britons did and developed a distinctive Christian culture. Irish missionaries would spread the faith from Scotland to Armenia, traveling prodigious distances, preaching, and observing and writing about their adventures. The fate of the island during at least part of the Dark Ages, however, was much the same as that of Britain: waves of savage raids by marauding seafarers, loss of life and ruin of homes and farms, the destruction of schools, churches, and libraries. We will visit this unique Celtic island and follow its extraordinary early Christian history.

The history of Ireland before its conversion is complex and much debated, partly because of the difficulties posed by those sources that still exist. Since there was never a Roman presence there, at least none that was recorded, we have none of those valuable chronicles penned by Roman travelers from the time of Julius Caesar on, so full of details about the non-Roman world. The Roman historian Tacitus provided some information about the place, possibly gained from Irish raiders captured by the Romans. He mentions Roman discussions about the feasibility of taking possession of the island, and how its division into many tribal areas would make conquest easy. The mapmaker Ptolemy had even produced a fairly accurate map of the island, rivers and all. Yet somehow the Romans never got around to making the attempt, perhaps because they knew what tenacious fighters the Irish raiders were and were loath to invade a country full of them.

We do know that Irish society was rural, hierarchical, and organized into clans or kinship groups. Local kings ruled the areas into which the island was divided. The Irish were seafarers who possessed a fleet, as St. Patrick was to learn—at first to his sorrow and later for his glory. The transmission of laws, stories, and history was carried on by the bards, or poets, who were honored and respected. Early Irish religion seems to have permeated daily life, with its sun-worship and numerous sacred customs, places, trees, and wells; there were gods and goddesses to be worshiped, and a priestly hierarchy of Druids. It is possible that human sacrifice was sometimes practiced, as it was in many primitive religions, though how common it was is unclear. There was at least one huge idol decorated with precious metals, which Patrick later destroyed.

Exactly when Christianity came to Ireland is unclear because of the many and varied stories about its presence there in early Christian times. There are legends about St. Paul or St. James preaching to the Irish, and individual Christians with Irish-sounding names—some of them martyrs—are found on the continent of Europe during the persecutions of the Church. Whether or not they were Irish is far from certain. When Pope St. Celestine, who was busy fighting the Pelagian heresy, found time to consecrate a deacon named Palladius and send him off to Ireland in the fifth century as a missionary bishop, he apparently sent him "to the Irish believing in Christ"; the scholar Bollandus wrote that the new bishop probably found more Christians in Ireland than he made.[23] We would like to know much more than we do about this intrepid man, but there was more than one Palladius in the mid-fifth century and some sources mix them up and attribute various achievements to the wrong one. It is possible that the Roman deacon Palladius who persuaded Germanus to visit Britain to fight Pelagianism is the one we want. If he was concerned about the Church in Britain he may have been interested in the pagan Irish as well. In any case, there is a record of Pope Celestine sending a new bishop named Palladius off to Ireland in the year 431.

Palladius and his companions—for he would not have gone alone—did not stay long in Ireland, possibly an indication that at least the part of the country in which they landed was already Christian. On the other hand, the short visit could have reflected an obdurate resistance on the part of pagans elsewhere on the island; we find mention of one particularly hostile chieftain. Very little is definite in this unsatisfactory story, but certainly Palladius did make at least some converts and build several churches. Why he did not stay longer is an intriguing question; some sources say he simply decided it was futile to remain in such an unwelcoming environment. Since we cannot know the reason for his early departure with any certainty, we will move on to St. Patrick. We know lots more about him. Meanwhile, Palladius moved on to Scotland, where it seems he later died. We hope he had more success with the Scots.[24]

Ireland's Patron Saint

In the years between Palladius and Patrick, who was born about 385 somewhere in Britain (or possibly Wales) into a Roman

---

[23] MacManus, pp. 103-104.

[24] Moran, "St. Palladius," *The Catholic Encyclopedia*, vol. 11.

Christian family, there does not seem to have been another missionary to the Irish. At the age of about 16 Patrick was captured by Irish raiders and taken to Ireland as a slave—a rude change of status for the son of an upper-class Roman governmental family such as his. He spent, according to his own detailed account, six years as a swineherd before he was able to make his escape and return to his family. Sometime later he began his studies for the priesthood and was ordained. He was haunted by the thought of the pagan people he had left behind, and in a dream he heard the voices of children calling him to Ireland.

At length he was consecrated a bishop and, after a series of delays and humiliations into which we will not go here, was commissioned to lead a mission to Ireland. It was a spectacular success, though it was not accomplished without hostility on the part of some of the Irish and even occasional violence against Patrick. He seems to have had enough energy for 10 missionaries. He was here, there, and everywhere: debating Druids, preaching to crowds, discussing poetry with the bards, and dealing with suspicious (and superstitious) local chieftains.[25]

Patrick also rewrote Irish laws to incorporate Christian principles, for example empowering poor men to compel nobles to pay a debt, and making the king himself answerable to the law.

---

[25] According to a pious tradition, one such chieftain sent the saint a cauldron as a gift and possibly also as a symbol of a land grant. When the servant delivered the pot, Patrick, who was always busy and short on time, said what he always said when anything, whether good or ill, came his way, *Gratias agamus*—"Let us give thanks," but he said it very quickly. When the servant returned, his master asked him eagerly what the saint had said. "He said, 'Gratzakam,'" was the reply. "Gratzakam? Is that all? Sounds like a spell!" And the servant was dispatched to recover the cauldron from its ungrateful recipient. After he had toiled back to his master with the thing, he was asked what the ingrate had said *this* time. "He said, 'Gratzakam,'" was the answer. "Gratzakam again! Hmm, must be a powerful spell if it's used for both the getting and the losing! Better give him back his cauldron." The overworked servant's reaction is not recorded.

Naturally, he established churches and monasteries all around the island.

As with St. Martin of Tours, miracles were also a necessary component of Patrick's evangelism, because of the "black magic" practiced by his pagan adversaries. Soon after his arrival in Ireland, for example, Patrick and his companions built a large paschal fire on Easter eve. The local king, learning of it, was furious because no fires were supposed to be lit until the Druids had lit theirs. Off the magicians were sent to extinguish Patrick's fire and himself with it. They failed in both tasks. Hauled before the king, Patrick was able to counter the seeming miracles of the pagan priests with wonders of his own. At one point the sorcerers conjured up a thick darkness but were unable to get rid of it; Patrick airily did so, remarking, "They can bring darkness but they cannot bring light."[26] Later an arch-Druid was lifted up into the air, like Simon Magus long before him, but when Patrick prayed, he was dashed to the ground. Another time a furious pagan chief raised his sword to smite the saint, only to find that his arm became paralyzed in mid-air and stayed that way until he submitted to Patrick. The incident changed him so much that he took instructions in the faith and became Patrick's devout disciple.

There is more, much more, but these few examples of what Patrick was up against illustrate the hold that Satan had over the pagan Irish priesthood and through them over the whole land. They also indicate the extraordinary means by which the country was at last won for Christ; in those times when hell is mysteriously allowed great power over nature and men, and preaching alone cannot defeat it, God gives extraordinary powers to his saints. Patrick's prodigies are a stunning reminder of this. By the time he died, on March 17, 493, the whole island was Catholic. An old Irish poem put it this way: "There was a demon at the

---

[26] MacManus, p. 115.

butt of every grass-blade in Eirinn before thy advent; but at the butt of every grass-blade in Eirinn today there is an angel."[27]

A Missionary People for the Dark Ages

Unlike the work of the Church in other pagan areas, the conversion of Ireland was accomplished peacefully: There were no Catholic martyrs in Ireland before the English came. With the faith, and especially with the monasteries, came literacy and learning, which the Irish welcomed wholeheartedly. They showed an extraordinary love for monasticism, which in Ireland was noted for its rigor and purity of life, and vocations flourished. The speech of the Irish reflected this esteem for the monastic life; the pope was referred to as "the abbot of Rome," and Christ was "the abbot of the Heavenly City." They also showed an amazing zeal for evangelization. No sooner were they converted than many of the Irish became themselves missionaries and set off for Britain, Brittany, Scotland, and possibly even Iceland. (When the Vikings arrived there in the seventh century it was said that Irish monks had beaten them to it.) The accounts of St. Brendan's voyages to Newfoundland in the late sixth century used to be considered legends, until replicas of his ships were built a few years ago and the voyage repeated successfully.

Other Irish missionaries went to France, where around the year 600 St. Columbanus and his companions rebuilt a monastery destroyed by the Huns, possibly Luxeuil, which became one of the great monastic schools of the Dark Ages. They went on to revive monasticism in Italy and elsewhere. Columba, a few decades earlier, had founded the almost legendary island monastery of Iona that flourished until—like so much that was beautiful, valuable, and pleasing to God—it was destroyed in the Reformation. I cannot resist a story, perhaps a true one, that is told about Columba. The son of a local Irish king, he became a monk. While visiting another monastery he saw a precious

---

[27] MacManus, pp. 125-126.

book of which he wanted to make a copy for his own monks. He asked permission of the abbot and was refused. Undaunted, Columba spent the remaining nights of his visit slipping into the library and copying the book—until he was caught by the abbot. Columba claimed that the copy belonged to him and the abbot declared that it must remain in his monastery's library. The case was put to the high king, who at first was somewhat nonplused. At length he fell back on an agricultural analogy familiar to him: "To every cow belongs her calf," he said. "So to every book belongs its copy."

Brother Columba had lost, and suddenly he was Prince Columba in a rage. He persuaded the chieftains of his clan to make war upon the high king and they did: the War of the Book, something only the Irish would declare. Columba's side won and he himself was offered the position of high king, his supreme temptation.

He was then overcome with repentance for his worldliness, abandoned the world once more and vowed to convert all the pagans in the country. But there were no pagans left in Ireland, so he sailed off to find some and convert them, along the way founding over a hundred churches. His beloved Iona was partially destroyed by Protestants in 1561, something he apparently foresaw. In one of his poems (for he was a poet too) he wrote, "In Iona of my heart, Iona of my love, instead of monks' voices shall be lowing of cattle. But ere the world come to an end, Iona shall be as it was."

Thus the converted Irish returned the favor of the great blessing given them by traveling in every direction on their own missionary journeys; from Germany to Africa, Iceland to Palestine, they brought back Christianity where it had been lost and planted it where it had never been. The Irish who stayed at home, in their monasteries or their schools, became great scholars, poets, and producers of glorious illuminated books like the Book of Kells (also called, interestingly, the Book of Columba, although it was made after his time). Saints and scholars indeed!

Had the Irish remained sunk in their paganism and the dark magic, the multitude of souls that Irish missionaries brought to the faith would also have remained under the tyranny of Satan, at least until other missionaries reached them, if they ever had. As it was, not only did the converted Irish become great apostles throughout the West and beyond they also became so imbued with the love of their religion that they were given the grace to remain faithful to death in the terrible trials that the distant future would bring upon them. In the case of the England, though it flourished as one of the great Catholic nations of the Middle Ages, there remained a certain latent tension between Church and state and between royal power and papal authority, even in medieval times. This subtle weakening of faith, along with a growing worldliness and nationalism, would end in its tragic rejection of the Church. Two nations, both originally Catholic, one long under the domination of the other: one faithful to its conversion and the other not. Yet it was all in God's providence, and his will that both should again share the faith remains unchanged.

ೞ Instruments of Conversion ಚ

The Temporal Sword

From this time onward we note a new instrument of conversion, one that we may be rather more reluctant to credit. That instrument is war.

Time and again we will see great Catholic leaders such as Charlemagne obliged to go to battle against pagan enemies, with the defeat of those enemies generally leading to their ultimate conversion. In other cases, the enemies are repulsed and retreat without being converted, but they are at least prevented from doing harm to the Church and the faithful. Among God's instruments for the preservation of the converted and the forced submission of future converts, then, we must number the great Catholic military warriors along with the spiritual ones.

Central and Eastern Europe: A.D. 800-1300

Charlemagne converted the Saxons 8th century

SCANDINAVIA

Vikings & Norsemen converted 10th-12th centuries

SAXONY

POLAND

Kiev ●

FRISIA

St. Willibrord 8th century

● Krakow

St. Stanislaw martyred 1079 †

HOLY ROMAN EMPIRE

MORAVIA

Sts. Cyril & Methodius preached to the Slavs 8th century

BAVARIA

St. Boniface 8th century

Magyars arrive 9th century

PANNONIA

BALKANS

Croats & Serbs converted 8th century

Constantinople
Great Schism: 1054

4

Barbarians of the Borderlands

The conversion of Ireland, England, and Gaul, along with other for-
mer provinces of the Roman Empire, might appear as both a very solid
achievement and a fine—even spectacular—prelude to Christianity's
spread throughout the world. In fact, the newly converted regions were
in a most precarious position in the centuries that followed the fall of
Rome. The example of many of the eastern Christian lands conquered
by Islam, where the faith virtually ceased to exist, served as a warning: If
the predatory tribes of central and eastern Europe remained pagan they
would put fledgling Christendom in grave peril. Their conversion, then,
was essential to the survival of the faith in Europe and its future success
among all nations.

The violent incursions of the Magyars (Hungarians) into
Europe from the east in the ninth century occurred at about
the same time that Viking raids were terrorizing the continent
from the north and west. It was not much good fleeing to the
south either, because of the Muslim fleets raiding the Mediterranean coast. Conditions in Italy were frequently chaotic, and the
state of the papacy—with unworthy popes, disputed elections,
and worse—was often appalling. No wonder we use the term
"Dark Ages" for the period from about the sixth through the
10th centuries—though not everything in that period was grim,
as we have seen. Certainly the empire of Charlemagne was a
great blessing for civilization in the late eighth to the mid-ninth
century, and we saw many good things happening during the
same period in England and Ireland. Still, the menace of invasion
was always there. In the late ninth century people could reason-
ably ask themselves when the next wave of raiders would come
from Scandinavia. Would the Arabs invade in force as they had
in Spain? What about the savage groups that had already come

from the east, like the Huns and the Avars? Were there more bloodthirsty nomads even now moving across the great steppe lands toward Europe? (There were.)

We are going to meet those invaders, leaving Catholic Ireland and crossing Europe to St. Martin's birthplace of Pannonia, near the Danube. On the way, we will note what had been going on in Europe while we were busy in England and Ireland. What had happened to the many different peoples within the realm of the Franks? Had all those converted pagans remained Christian? What of the peoples just outside its borders? We will also look in some detail at those outposts of Christian spirituality, civilization, and progress that were the monasteries. They deserve more than cursory attention because of the key role they played in many areas of life in the Dark Ages—including some that the monks themselves never dreamed they would have to deal with.

We can pass quickly through Francia, where we have already been. The decadent Merovingians ruled in the sixth and seventh centuries until their peaceful removal by competent mayors of the palace and the eventual reign of Charlemagne. The rulers of both the western and eastern Frankish lands had to contend with Viking raids such as those that devastated Ireland and England; it must have seemed to the populace of northern and western Europe that there was a limitless supply of warriors being hatched in Scandinavia, so many and so costly were the attacks.

The main linguistic division of the realm was between speakers of Romance languages—Latin-based tongues such as French and Italian—and those who spoke one of the Germanic tongues. This was not just a difference of language but of culture that languages bring with them, and those cultures would mark the new political entities that would emerge from the great Charles's realm.

Preaching to the Peoples of the North

Frisia was the name given to the Germanic coastal areas bordering the North Sea (it would later be called the Netherlands) not far from England; in fact, some Frisians had settled in eastern England in the fifth or sixth centuries. In the seventh century there was an English monk and bishop, St. Wilfrid, who seems to have spent most of his life in a rather tumultuous career that included several visits to Rome on pilgrimage or ecclesiastical business. On one of these expeditions he landed in Frisia, where he stopped and preached to the people there, apparently with spectacular success—converting, according to his biographer, almost the entire population of the region in which he landed. He did not stay long, returning to England where for good measure he converted pagan Sussex before dying in 709. But he had aroused interest in Frisia among other English missionaries.

One of these was his disciple St. Willibrord, who in turn went to Frisia and achieved a great deal there, founding monasteries and training and ordaining clergy. On one of his trips to Rome he was consecrated bishop of the Frisians, and after building a church in Utrecht, which he made his cathedral, he was known as bishop of Utrecht. Somewhere he found time to lead a mission to what is now Luxembourg, south of Frisia, where there seems to have been a small monastery on the site of a former Roman villa in the town of Echternach. When Willibrord arrived in 698, the abbess of the place deeded to him an abbey, chapel, lands, animals, and tenants; the gift was enlarged later by royal grant. From this base, the energetic Willibrord proceeded to convert— or in some cases reconvert—the people of Luxembourg. He attacked the vestiges of paganism that he found, destroying pagan shrines and combating pagan customs, sometimes by clever substitution. Thus he countered the cult of a woman, possibly a nature goddess, by introducing devotion to the Blessed Virgin Mary. An almost casual miracle-worker, this *Salvator Luxemburgensium* is credited with quashing the plague of 718. Following the example of St. Martin in France, he divided the country into parishes.[28] He is still much beloved of the Luxembourgeois, and

---

[28] Rousseau, p. 4.

you can still drink the water of the miraculous spring associated with him in the basilica of Echternach and venerate the tomb where he was laid to rest many years later.

Before that rest, however, Willibrord returned to Frisia, where for three years he traveled on missionary journeys. Here is one of those instances of reconversion that we find when an original conversion either did not penetrate souls deeply, when armed resistance managed to drive out the faith, or when the attraction of former pagan ways proved too strong. In Frisia, it had certainly seemed that the work begun by Willibrord's mentor and predecessor, Wilfrid, had been completed. In 716, however, one Duke Radbod, hostile to Christianity, came to power in Frisia and set about destroying monasteries and churches, setting up temples once more and killing missionaries. Willibrord and his companions managed to escape, returning when that unpleasant ruler died three years later. They then restored what he had destroyed and razed the pagan shrines and temples that he had built. In 719 the young St. Boniface joined Willibrord for three years, learning much from him, no doubt, before going on to his own adventures among the Germans.

In the meantime, there were to the north the pagan and unruly Danes, of unsavory reputation. Willibrord was brave enough to pay a visit to the Danish king and investigate the prospects for missionary work in his land. These were far from promising, and having made no progress and no converts, the saint returned south. He was now advanced in years and must have been exhausted from his strenuous life; he retired to his beloved monastery of Echternach, where he died on November 7, 739. He had a reputation for friendliness to all as well as for miracle-working, and sometimes for both together. It was said that once when he was visiting the monastery at Echternach he checked the monks' cells to make sure they had everything they needed, and then proceded to the cellars. There he found only a little wine left in one of the casks. He put his staff into the cask, no doubt asked God for what he wanted, and left the monastery. When the cellarer entered the wine room the next day, he found the cask full to overflowing. Running after Willibrord he went down on his knees, stammering his thanks and praise of the miracle. The saint sent him home, warning him to keep quiet about it. This sort of thing happened so often during Willibrord's life that it is no wonder he was venerated as a saint even before his death.

The Apostle to the Germans

Boniface, whose original name was Winfrid, is yet another great fruit of that missionary harvest produced by the conversion of England and Ireland. He was born in Wessex and became, like so many other missionaries of the time, a Benedictine monk. He was a talented teacher and preacher, but he heard the stories brought back by missionaries of the great need for apostles to the German tribes, and being one was his earnest desire. He finally gained permission and went off to the continent, first traveling to Rome to obtain authorization from the pope and then turning north, to find the German pagans he longed to convert.

The first areas through which he traveled, Bavaria and Al-emannia, were already Christian. So was Thuringia, or at least so Boniface had been told. But when he arrived in this northeast-ern section of Germany, he found much different conditions. St. Kilian, his Irish missionary predecessor, had managed to convert a duke of Thuringia and his son, but they had been murdered— possibly because they were too zealous about spreading their new religion. Boniface tried to persuade what Christians he was able to find to practice their faith more earnestly, and he did make a few converts. Still, he was a not a success, and somewhat at a loss, he set out to consult the ruler of the Franks, Charles Martel. Along the way he spent some time with Willibrord in Frisia, as we have seen, and after returning to Rome to be or-dained bishop, decided once more to try to make a dent in the resistance of the Thuringians.

Boniface found that the religious situation in Thuringia had become a mishmash of Christianity, superstition, and heterodox practices; possibly this was due to some earlier Celtic missionaries, armed with more zeal than learning, who had sowed such confusion that many of the so-called Catholics saw no contradiction in assisting at Mass in the morning and consulting an oracle or visiting a pagan shrine in the afternoon. Indeed, a deep-seated fascination with witchcraft, paganism, and sorcery seems to have been widespread in Thuringia. The bishop of a neighboring diocese was hostile to boot, apparently viewing Boniface as an intruder on his territory.

Boniface wrote letters home, and others to Charles Martel, asking for help. His friends pitched in; they sent books and advice, and a number of them, both men and women, came to be his assistants. Things got a little better, and Boniface was able to build churches, chapels, and even monasteries and convents. Still, he wrote a letter to Rome to explain that the work was too much for one man and a few volunteers and that he needed more substantial reinforcements. In reply he received only praise for his efforts. He next went to Rome in person to inform the pope that he wished to resign his office and concentrate on the Saxons instead. The Holy Father would not hear of it, and Boniface trudged back across the Alps, this time as archbishop for all of Germany. In Bavaria he began the work of reform: ferreting out invalid ordinations, appointing new bishops, and regularizing and revitalizing dioceses and religious houses.

He also presided over the first German synod, in 742, and it is worth looking at, since the issues it dealt with provide a glimpse of the state of the Church and society in the eighth century. It forbade clerics to bear arms or take part in wars, which some of them had apparently been doing with zest and frequency, and as a symbol of their separation from the world they were ordered to wear a long black garment—likely the chasuble or cassock. They were also forbidden to hunt, probably because it was too time-consuming an activity, possibly because it was not seemly for clerics to shed the blood of any creature. As for the recently converted Germans, prone to return to their superstitions and pagan worship: "We ordain that every bishop, within the limits of his own diocese, forbid all heathen superstition, such as sacrifices to the shades of the dead, spells, charms, the immolation of victims, and the sacrilegious fires."[29]

Another major headache for Boniface, apart from stubborn paganism and armed priests, was widespread ignorance among both laity and clergy. The cultivation of learning had lapsed to such a degree that priests were even garbling the words used in administering the sacraments. Boniface actually wrote to Pope Zachary asking whether a baptism was valid if administered with this meaningless formula: *Ego te baptizo in nomine Patria, et Filia, et Spiritua Sancta.* ("I baptize you in the name country, daughter, and the holy [meaningless word] *spiritua.*") Wise Pope Zachary replied that such a baptism, administered in the name of the Trinity and with the intention of doing what the Church does, would be valid; mere ignorance of the language would not render it invalid.

Ignorance and heresy could go hand in hand, however, as when a Scots priest in Germany started teaching that baptism was a worthless formality and a German priest insisted that men "under the earth" (apparently meaning on the other side from him) were not redeemed by Christ.[30] This is but a small sample of what the Church was up against in the Dark Ages: It had not only to convert pagans (and make those conversions stick) but to foster political order and public morality while promoting literacy and education everywhere. The amazing thing is that the Church actually did all this. It just took time, and it would take the lives of numerous martyrs.

When St. Willibrord died, Boniface took temporary charge of his old friend's diocese. Much of his later life, in fact, seems to have been spent in administration rather than in the missionary journeys and convert-making he had always longed for. Finally,

---

[29] D'Arras, vol. 2, pp. 328-329.
[30] Ibid., 230-231.

in 754, when he must have been about 75 years old and having duly consecrated his successor, he resigned his office and set off again for Frisia, which seems to have been always ready to convert and just as ready to relapse and massacre its converters. He met with initial success, but when he returned in 755 to administer confirmation to the new Catholics, pagans appeared suddenly and murdered St. Boniface, along with dozens of his converts and helpers.

Boniface had expressed a wish that he be buried at the famous monastery of Fulda, which had been founded under his supervision and to which he returned every year for a few days of prayer and meditation, as well as to instruct the monks. His wish was granted.

The German World in the Ninth Century

We have seen some of the troubles Boniface faced in dealing with the German regions, even though they had supposedly been Christianized long before he got there. We noted also that he had yearned to go to the pagan Saxons and convert them, though he never managed it. Here we will look at a drastic solution to the Saxon problem, one that the Church rejects as a matter of principle but nevertheless was the only thing that worked in this case.

That Charlemagne ruled a largely Christian empire was due both to his own promotion of missionary activity and to the previous conversion of many of his subjects. The Saxons were the stubborn exception. As Einhard, a biographer of the great emperor, put it, the Saxons were a "fierce people, given to the worship of devils, and hostile to our religion." They "did not consider it dishonorable to transgress and violate all law, human and divine," and having been subdued time and time again they would routinely violate terms and return to their murderous ways.[31]

---

[31] Perry, p. 203.

As a last resort, having suffered so much from Saxon raids and crimes, Charlemagne took an unusual step, offering the Saxons peace and integration into the empire in return for their conversion to Christianity. Now, the Church has always condemned forced conversion; what are we to make of this? Some Catholic commentators have argued that the case of the Saxons presented unique difficulties for Charlemagne and his people. They had a reputation for killing priests, looting monasteries, and sacrificing prisoners to their gods. Treaties had been tried and broken. Conversion by persuasion had been tried, making many martyrs and very few Saxon Christians. The lives and the safety of all the king's subjects were at stake here, and something clearly had to be done to tame the Saxons. They were required, under the threat of another war and possible annihilation, to agree that missionaries could freely move among them preaching the gospel. Their agreement to this would not simply spare their lives but bring them the considerable benefits—economic as well as cultural—of membership in the great Carolingian Empire. Possibly they had never actually paid attention to what Christianity was all about, but they were about to learn.

The Saxons' receptivity to the good news may well have astonished their conquerors, since conversion seems to have gone surprisingly fast. Missionaries went out among them and preached, built churches, and introduced Christian practices. There was apparently some deplorable harshness in the enforcement of adherence to the new faith, such as when Charlemagne was said to have executed thousands of Saxons for backsliding. It does not sound like him, but if it happened it was a crime that must have set back the cause of true conversion. And yet by the following century the Saxon nation seems to have been so thoroughly converted that the Saxons were sending missionaries of their own to the pagans of the east. The saying that God writes straight with crooked lines certainly seems to fit here. A wild and vicious people, who seemed unreachable by ordinary missionary methods, was compelled by force to listen to the truth and ended by not only accepting it but also exporting it to others who still dwelt in the darkness.

The Borderlands of the Empire: Scandinavia

Charlemagne's empire had included most of what we consider Europe today, with the major exceptions of Spain, Scandinavia, and southern Italy. By the late ninth century, it no longer existed, except as an elusive ideal. Charles's grandsons and their sons divided and subdivided the vast territory, and the borders of their various realms changed so frequently that it must have been hard for the inhabitants to keep up with who their current rulers were. These rulers were known by blunt, plain names: Charles the Bald, Charles the Fat, Charles the Simple. "The Bad" and "the Mad" sometimes occurred too, and poor Louis the Stammerer was not allowed to forget his disability. Among all the Carolingian successors, however, there is no "Great"—*Carolus Magnus* was unrepeatable. In the following century, the Carolingian line dynasty died out in both main sections of that realm and was succeeded in France by the Capetian line and in Germany by a dynasty of those formerly vicious, now Christian, but always enduring Saxons, who would produce more than one king for Germany. The Franks, both French and German, were now within the Catholic Church and within the cultural framework that the Church brought with it. There were many tribes still unconverted and uncivilized that needed to be brought into Christendom and, as long as they remained outside it, posed a constant threat to its existence.

Throughout the Dark Ages, both church and state were particularly concerned with the conversion of the Scandinavian kingdoms, the homelands of all those invaders who had made life so miserable for most of Christian Europe. The Church naturally hoped to save the souls of the terrorists of the time, while the rulers of lands ravaged by them hoped that Christianity would make them peaceful enough to want to stay home. In the ninth century they were far from doing that. In the early decades of the century Swedish Vikings ventured as far as Constantinople, returning in 860 to mount an attack on the city. It failed, but it was a warning to the Byzantines that danger to their empire lay even to the north (they were well aware of dangers to the south, east, and west).

A few years earlier, a Danish lord known to history as Rurik had led an expedition down the rivers of Russia to Novgorod, where he founded a state that subsequently expanded southward. These *Rus* intermarried with the Slavic population and formed the first Russian state. Some of Rurik's men went further south to what is now Ukraine, establishing Kiev, where according to legend the apostle Andrew had visited and erected a cross around the year 55.[32] These new states would receive Christianity in its Greek form, from Constantinople, and would in later centuries follow their mother Church into unhappy schism. In the ninth century the great missionary brothers Sts. Cyril and Methodius, who did so much to bring the Slavic peoples out of paganism, visited Ukraine. They were the first to devise an alphabet for the languages of the people they met, thus facilitating the development of a literary Slavic language, which would also be used for the liturgy, known as Old Church Slavonic.

The conversion of Kiev accelerated around 988 when Prince Vladimir was baptized. His grandmother had been a Christian, though he himself was a thoroughgoing pagan who, according to some sources, resorted to occasional human sacrifice. After his baptism he was determined to promote Christianity among his people and was pretty heavy-handed about it. Perhaps it was the right approach, since Ukrainian paganism seems to have been deep-rooted and stubbornly resistant to the progress of the faith—resembling the Saxon version in its tenacity. Western missionaries were also active in the country in the following century, and gradually paganism disappeared—or at least became much less visible.

---

[32] Halecki, pp. 32-33.

By the 12th century, missionaries had built dioceses in Norway, Sweden, and Denmark, but the old Vikings and Norsemen were slow to become real, practicing Christians. Although the Scandinavians produced saints by martyring the missionaries sent to them, they seem to have generated few of their own. History records a handful of Danish saints, including the eleventh-century King St. Canute IV, a stern and upright ruler who promoted the interests of the Church in his realm. He nearly led an expedition in 1085 against the Normans who had taken over England in 1066 (the Norman Conquest). That came to nothing and the following year, in the course of a widespread revolt, the king, his brother, and some companions were martyred in a church where they were praying.

In that same 11th century, Norway could claim its own royal saint and martyr, Olaf Haraldson. He may have been baptized sometime between 998 (when he would have been three years old) and 1010, but that did not stop his career as one of those Viking pirates who brought such grief to England. He must have gone to sea as a young teenager; possibly it was during the course of his English campaigns that he began to take Christianity seriously.

In any case, when he became king of Norway in 1015, at the age of 20, he promoted the faith zealously and brought English priests and bishops to Norway to assist him. His religious and political reforms made enemies, and a revolt, assisted by King Canute of England and Denmark, uncle of St. Canute, brought exile to Olaf and the crown of Norway to Canute. After Olaf returned two years later with an army and died in battle against the rebels, reports began to spread of miraculous events occurring during the conflict and, later, around his incorrupt body. His cult developed rapidly and spread far beyond Norway.

At the same time, Christianity had also begun to make progress in Sweden, where a Swede named Botvid, who had been converted in England, returned to his country as a missionary around the year 1100. By the 14th century the Church in

Sweden had matured sufficiently to produce St. Bridget—wife, mother, mystic, founder of a religious order, and one of the patron saints of Europe. She is known for her visions and revelations, and certain forms of prayer attributed to her, considered particularly efficacious, have been widely practiced over the centuries. Her daughter Catherine was also a saint and during the Great Schism would travel to Rome to testify in favor of the rightful claimant to the papacy.

Finland, sparsely populated by both migrating Finnish tribes and Swedish colonists, may have had some exposure to Christianity as early as the 11th century. The country had suffered from Viking attacks, however, and it was not until the Swedes themselves had been converted that they made a real effort to convert their former victims. In 1157, King Erik of Sweden went to Finland to begin the job of both conquest and conversion, accompanied by one Bishop Henrick—who was martyred the following year, as was his successor. During one hard-fought battle the king was said to have asked a sign from God, and both he and his army saw a golden cross appear against the blue sky. They won the battle, and today that emblem appears on the Swedish flag. Erik was known for his just and wise rule, as well as for care of the poor and the sick. He was at Mass one day in May 1160, the day after Ascension, when he was informed that a pagan Danish army was on its way to assassinate him. "Let us at least finish the sacrifice," he replied. "The rest of the feast I shall keep elsewhere." He met his enemies as he was leaving the church and died at their hands.

The Russian Orthodox had also made some attempts to convert the Finns from the east, with little success. From the 13th through the 15th centuries a series of bishops, both foreign-born and ethnic Finns, built churches and established libraries and religious houses, which would seem to indicate the existence of a thriving Catholic culture. In 1523, however, the election of Eric Svenonis as bishop was not confirmed by Rome and he resigned: the last Catholic bishop of Finland. The king appointed one of his favorites, who began to force Lutheranism upon Finnish Catholics by deception and threats of expulsion or death for those clerics who resisted. (This is certainly an early example of Protestant persecution of Catholics, considering that Luther only got going in 1517.) Martyrs there were in Finland, and in one place all the monks in a monastery were hanged. By the following century, Finnish Catholicism barely existed, and the country now has the smallest number of Catholics of any nation in Europe.

We may pause here to ponder the historical significance of the conversion of the various Slavic tribes, or of the Scandinavian peoples, or of any of the others whose stories we have been following. Many of these peoples, and their descendents in other parts of the world, are not Catholic now, so what is the point? What difference did their conversion actually make? It can be argued that conversion to the true faith is the most important event in any nation's history. It marks that state as part of Christendom, with a distinct national vocation. Even in the case of the countries that have apostatized—Scandinavia, for example, is today one of the least observant regions of the Christian West— the fact of their calling remains, along with the hope that they will return to it someday.

On the practical level, integration into Christendom, if it did not always bring political peace, brought an institution that worked tirelessly to achieve that peace: the Church. The conversion of Scandinavia meant the cessation of Viking attacks, which in turn meant that defense expenditures that had drained the neighboring states for centuries could be used productively. Conversion of the Slavs meant the possibility of peaceful overland travel for merchants, explorers, and missionaries between eastern and western Europe and between Europe and Asia. A Christian state traded with other Christian states, often at great international fairs; it had the benefit of schools, libraries, orphanages, hospitals, and other institutions brought by the Church. This happy state of affairs did not last long in some areas; the Mongol empire would loom in the east later in the Middle Ages, along with the Turkish onslaught from the south. Even then, however, Christianity would see her people through those attacks, and later inspire them—in the case of the Russian revolt against the Mongols and of the west against the Turks—to fight back. Conversion mattered; where it did not last long, reconversion may yet come in God's good time.

The Slavic Borderlands

To the east, southeast, and northeast of Charlemagne's empire there were also Slavic tribes; not only the Russians and Ukrainians, whose states were founded by Vikings and who were converted from Byzantium, but close to a dozen other ethnically Slavic groups. Leaving out those within the Russian sphere, such as most of the Slavs of the Balkan Peninsula except for the Croats (and the Bosnians, who would end up largely Muslims), and ignoring arcane quarrels over where they all came from, we are going to deal with four main groups of people whom we will cautiously call "Slavs" and who were converted to Catholicism in the Dark Ages. These are the Poles, Croats, Slovenes, and Czechs. (The reader who wishes to know about the Red Ruthenians will have to look elsewhere. We can only do so much.)

The Poles

In Poland we find yet another region into which Charlemagne's successors decided to extend their empire. Like the rest of Europe, which was settled in prehistoric times by previously nomadic tribes who finally developed a more stable, agricultural way of life, Polish tribal units had settled in what is now Poland, forming a state in the 10th century under their ruler Mieszko. When the Germans began to push east, Mieszko made an alliance with them and, in 966, agreed to accept Christianity and was baptized. Missionaries came to Poland from all over Europe, and soon churches, monasteries, and the culture of the West spread throughout the country. Prince Mieszko even declared himself a vassal of the pope, to whom he sent a yearly tribute. His son, Boleslaw Chrobry, developed a large army, expanded his territory, and had himself crowned king. Poland now had more prestige and power, but formal conversion seems to have left most of the population lukewarm Catholics at best, possibly because most of the clergy were foreigners.

There was little rapport between them and their flocks, and during an interregnum in the 11th century there was actually a series of violent revolts, mostly by rebellious peasants who murdered noblemen and clergy, destroyed monasteries and churches, and even, in one part of the country, restored paganism. There was also widespread resentment against increasing German domination of the government. In the middle of the century, an independent Polish Catholic kingdom emerged and implemented widespread reforms of Church and state, but resistance to reform by corrupt clerics, revolts, and political upheavals continued until the late Middle Ages. By the 15th century, with a native Polish clergy, education, cultural development, and agricultural progress—largely the result of instruction by the many monks and nuns who by then worked in the country—Poland had finally become a great Catholic power, furnishing the Church with hundreds of saints, many of them martyrs who were massacred by medieval pagan invaders, not to mention the victims of the Reformation (which failed in Poland), the Nazis, and the Communists.

One of those martyrs, St. Stanisław, became a priest in that violent and largely pagan 11th century, and was later made a bishop. He founded monasteries, brought in papal legates, and fulfilled all the duties of his office until there came a fatal interruption. He seems to have criticized the king's treatment of some soldiers and their wives, or, alternatively, supported some enemies of the king for some reason. Whatever the issue was, it caused the king to order his men to execute the troublesome bishop. (One is reminded of King Henry II of England and his archbishop, Thomas Becket; Becket too had the misfortune to stand against a king with a cruel temper.) The Polish king's men would not touch the bishop, so King Bolesław took matters into his own hands. He was said to have struck down Stanislaw at the altar, as he was saying Mass or, in another account, in the royal castle. He was hacked into pieces and thrown into a pool of water. The king was so disgraced that he fled to Hungary and was succeeded by his brother. This incident illustrates how strong the faith could be in newly converted states, strong enough to face a gruesome martyrdom. Stanisław and Becket were both loyal to their kings but to God first.

The Croats

As part of the waves of migration into the late Roman Empire, the Croats ended up on the coast of the Balkan Peninsula, where in the seventh century they and the Serbs were converted and baptized. The Serbs later became Orthodox, but the Croats maintained contacts with Charlemagne's empire, which occupied northern Croatia for a time, and the little state later became an independent kingdom. When the last Croatian king died in 1102, the crown was offered to Hungary on the condition that Croatian internal sovereignty be maintained. Several religious orders set up houses in the country, and Catholic culture and education flourished.[33]

The Slovenes

A little further to the north, in part of the Roman province of Pannonia, the Celtic settlers were swamped by a wave of Slavic migrants, and the resultant mixed population, eventually known as Slovenes, formed an entity known as Carantania. In the eighth century it was ruled by a duke who became a vassal of Bavaria, and it was from the Catholic Germans that the Slovenes first

---

[33] Krmpotic, "Croatia."

received missionaries and Catholic culture. Over the centuries, the lands of the Slovenes were conquered by invaders from the east, divided into pieces, and incorporated into the Holy Roman and Habsburg empires.

It should be mentioned that all the peoples we have met in this chapter would suffer from the attacks and occupation of the Ottoman Turks in the 15th and 16th centuries. The Christian nations of the Balkan Peninsula in particular suffered from the peculiarly cruel Turkish custom known as *devşirme*. The Turks would send army officers to Christian villages where the people were required to bring their young sons to the village square. The boys were scrutinized like animals by the Janissary officers, who looked for physical attractiveness as well as fitness and chose a certain number. The boys, whether teenagers destined for the army or little children intended to be raised and trained for other functions at the sultan's court, were forcibly circumcised and converted to Islam and then trained for whatever purpose they would serve. They would never see their families again. This was not a rare atrocity; it is estimated that half a million children were thus ripped from their homes during the seemingly endless Turkish onslaughts on Europe.[34]

The Czechs, our last Slavic people, were converted in the ninth century; the busy St. Methodius took part in their conversion and baptized a Bohemian duke. In the following century, paganism was still strong, and when the Christian ruler Wratislaw died, his pagan widow, Dragomir, became regent and, with her supporters, began to attack the Church. Her son Wenceslaus, however, had been raised a Christian and been much influenced by his grandmother and teacher, St. Ludmilla. He opposed his mother and her allies, took over the government, and became duke (not king, *pace* the Christmas carol) of Bohemia under German protection. (Ludmilla, meanwhile, was murdered for supporting her Catholic grandson.) From Germany, Wenceslaus

---

[34] Moczar, *Islam*, pp. 37–40.

brought missionaries who instituted the Latin rite of the Mass in place of the Eastern liturgy, which for some time had lacked priests trained in it.

Infuriated at the reforms of her son, Dragomir persuaded his brother to assassinate him, and the saintly duke was hacked to pieces and buried at the scene. Later, his brother repented of his crime and had the remains disinterred and taken to Prague, where they now lie in a magnificent tomb within St. Vitus Cathedral (which Wenceslaus had built) and are still much venerated. By the 13th and 14th centuries, the country seems to have stopped hacking up saints and developed a flourishing state—a golden age of Catholic culture. Too soon, though, the country was infected with the heretical ideas of John Wycliffe that were brought from England by royal travelers and taken up by Jan Hus, with tragic results for the Church. The nationalistic "proto-reformation" that developed around Hus led in the 16th century to the triumph of Protestantism.

Further to the east of Germany there were a number of regions inhabited by tribes who had either been there for several centuries or migrated in the late Roman period when they had fled the Huns. Among these were the Avars, a pagan tribe from the steppes that may have moved west in the wake of the Huns, settling temporarily on land vacated by them. Their ethnic roots are uncertain, since they seem to have mixed with Bulgars and other eastern European peoples in the course of their rather brief career. They first harried the empire in the sixth and seventh centuries and were driven back by the imperial armies. By the time of Charlemagne they were established more or less in the area of the old Roman province of Pannonia and surrounding areas, and there may have been for a time an actual Avar empire, with the Avars ruling the surrounding Slavs and Bulgars and causing the migration of other groups fleeing their attacks. They attacked Charlemagne's realm more than once. When he finally defeated them in 796 with the help of Slavic warriors, the question arose as to whether the Avars, like the Saxons, should be forced to accept Christianity. Fierce as they were, and apparently lovers of war, would anything less induce them to become a peaceful people? Charlemagne may have been inclined to force the issue, but Alcuin firmly disagreed. He wrote to his friend, the archbishop of Salzburg, whose jurisdiction would extend to the Avar realm, urging him to proceed gently and to forego in Pannonia the collecting of tithes, which had apparently rankled with the Saxons. He wrote the emperor on the same subject, discussing the type of missionaries who should be sent to the Avars and how they should proceed. Charlemagne apparently took Alcuin's advice and decided against compulsory baptism of the Avars. He seems to have gone even a little further, issuing milder provisions for the Saxons.[35] Meanwhile, the Avar chief had requested baptism, large numbers of his people followed him, and missionaries and teachers began to work in the Avar territory.

Here we have an example of the good results of a gentle approach to conversion. Despite the legendary ferocity of this people, they seem to have responded enthusiastically to the religion they were offered. There was, however, little time left for the Avars. A few years after 800 they were conquered and absorbed by the Bulgars and disappeared from history. They probably intermarried with Slavs and Bulgars until there was no Avar national identity left. Many of them must have died in the assaults of the Bulgars, which makes us realize how providential it was that they were given the faith just before they left history forever.

The Pagan Hungarians
Become a Catholic Nation

The Hungarians were another of that seemingly inexhaustible supply of tribes from the vast Eurasian steppe lands, like the Avars, Bulgars, and other nomadic peoples, though they came to have a distinctive destiny within Europe. Their origins are murky and have led some imaginative writers to posit ancient Egypt or

---

[35] Fletcher, pp. 221-222.

Sumeria as their original homeland. We need not get into that question, since our concern is how they became one of the great Catholic nations of Eastern Europe. Their own name for themselves is Magyars; they were dubbed "Hungarian" because, when they finally descended on Europe like a bomb that exploded in all directions, the terrified populace thought they were the Huns returning to repeat their horrifying fifth-century campaigns. (Attila, ironically, is a popular male name in modern Hungary.)

Of the centuries when these fierce horsemen wandered the steppes we have little information. Their religion seems to have been a type of shamanism and involved worship of the spirits of natural things. They seem to have believed in one god, whom they called Isten, as well as a variety of other spirits and creatures, including a great white stag that led them over the Carpathians and into their future homeland. Ethnically they were related to the distant Finns, and their unusual language shows influence from the Turks.

The Hungarians clashed with the Avars but were allied with another tribe, the Khazars, whose own conversion story is unique. Once they decided to renounce paganism, it seems they were solicited both by the Byzantines and the Muslims, the envoys of each religion angling for Khazar political support as well as Khazar souls, and their ruler felt threatened no matter which he chose. Then appeared, on unrelated business, an envoy of a Muslim ruler in Spain. This emissary happened to be a Jew, and he convinced the Khan that his religion was the one to choose. It was monotheistic, after all, but (and this may have been his chief selling point) there was no Jewish kingdom left to make awkward demands upon a leader who only wanted to be left in peace. That is how the Khazars became the unlikely "13th tribe" of Israel.

As for our Hungarians, they burst upon Europe in the late ninth century, crossing the Carpathians into Pannonia under the leadership of their almost legendary chief, Árpád, and used it as a base of operations after subduing the population. The ninth-century Hungarians seemed most unlikely candidates to become champions of the faith as they ruthlessly raided nearby areas. They looked quite different from their victims, with shaved heads and dark complexions, strange weapons, blood-curdling battle cries, and unfamiliar tactics. They were hard to engage as they sped through the land on horses, bringing death and devastation. Rumor had it that they were not merely the descendents of Attila and his Huns but the embodiment of the Gog and Magog foretold by Ezekiel, or something out of the Apocalypse.[36]

After they laid waste to Bavaria and Moravia, their activities appeared to subside—until they suddenly turned up in Italy, demolishing a Lombard defense force and at one point entering Rome itself. From 912 to 917, they confined themselves to ravaging German provinces, but then they crossed the Rhine. Soon they were in Burgundy, Lorraine, and southern France.[37] By this time Europeans everywhere were panicked at the rumors they heard of the return of the Huns. The Viking raids on the coasts made matters worse. People fleeing westward from the Magyars were in danger of falling victim to Scandinavian rapacity, and poor souls running from the Norsemen on the coasts found themselves and falling into the hands—or onto the swords—of the horsemen. They targeted monasteries, and many religious houses were looted and damaged, their inmates killed or scattered.

The Catholic Kingdom of Hungary

Meanwhile, in post-Carolingian eastern Germany, Prince Otto came to the throne in 936 at the age of 24 with the goal of nothing less than the restoration of the German empire. With the support of the Church, and despite revolts by some of the rulers of the numerous territories under his rule, Otto was able to achieve his dream of an empire worthy of Charlemagne—or

---

[36] D'Arras, II, p. 569.
[37] Ibid.

almost. Ironically, it was partly to the Hungarians that he owed his success. Some of the rebels against Otto's authority were rash enough (or stupid enough) to solicit help from the mighty Magyars, which was gladly given. Having sized up their temporary allies, by 954 they were raiding German provinces with abandon, drawing the attention of the rebel lords and allowing Otto to recover his throne.

The following year the Magyars attacked the city of Augsburg, which was ill equipped to resist such a force. Its bishop, St. Udalric, with no armor but his vestments, organized the defense of the city, encouraged the people, and stood on the walls all day, ignoring the darts and arrows of the enemy. (We recall Sts. Genevieve and Lupus, facing Attila the Hun 500 years earlier.) At the last moment, as the attackers were scaling the walls, Otto and his army arrived and saved the city. Later that same year, at the great Battle of Lechfeld, he decisively defeated the Magyar forces, which were forced to withdraw to Pannonia. According to legend, only seven members of the great army made it home.[38] We cannot follow the ups and downs, the wise and the not so wise policies of the very interesting ruler Otto—now Otto I, the Great, Holy Roman Emperor—because we must follow our own quarry trooping back to what would become far more than a base of military operations.

We have said that the Magyars were pagan, but there is some evidence that they had been exposed to Christianity in earlier centuries while they were still in the steppe lands. There were Nestorian missionaries in Asia and even Tibet, possibly as early as the fourth century, who may have encountered the Magyars, and the future Hungarians were probably in the area when the Khazars were pondering their choice of a new religion. In the 940s, in between raids, a Magyar leader named Bulcsu may have been baptized at Constantinople only to apostatize later, though the source for this whole episode is somewhat dubious. At least one

---

[38] McCartney, p. 11.

Magyar seems to have brought with him into Europe a shield made in the region of Levédia—to the east of the Urals—bearing a cross in its center and fashioned in the Byzantine style.[39] When the Magyars finally settled down for good in what would become their permanent home territory, they encountered the Latin form of Christianity through contact with the Catholic Slavs who were already there.

They were not, however, in a great hurry to adopt it. It was some 15 years after the defeat at Lechfeld that the Magyar ruler Géza, great-grandson of Árpád, began to cultivate friendly relations with the court of Emperor Otto and with Bavaria and to allow missionaries to come to his country. The chronicler Liudprand comments acidly that until then the barbaric Hungarians had responded to *Kyrie eleison* by uttering "the diabolic and vicious cry, *huj-huj*."[40] They must have irritated their neighbors in more ways than one.

Géza's son Vajk had been baptized with the Christian name of Stephen, possibly by St. Adelbert of Prague,[41] and it was he who came to the throne when his father died in 996. St. Stephen, canonized in 1083, would become "the best-beloved, most famous and perhaps the most important figure in Hungarian history."[42] At the beginning of his great reign in the year 1000, Pope Sylvester II sent him a crown and an apostolic cross. Stephen formally consecrated his country to the Blessed Virgin Mary, the first monarch to do so. Nevertheless, the conversion of Hungary was not a simple task. Presenting the faith to the Magyar mentality does not seem to have been the difficulty; the Magyars already had a surprisingly large vocabulary of spiritual terms—in addition to their ancient word for God—that could

---

[39] Szántó, p. 310.

[40] Bakay, p. 546.

[41] Ibid., p. 547.

[42] Ibid., p. 12.

be used for Christian concepts.[43] Rather, there seems to have been resentment against the foreign missionaries who came into the country in large numbers, as well as a reluctance to give up immemorial pagan practices and dismiss the lesser spirits to which they were attached. One chief considering baptism, when told he would have to renounce multiple gods, was said to have huffed, "I can afford more than one."

In 1046, the famous missionary St. Gerard (Gellert) was martyred by being thrown from the hill that now bears his name into the Danube below.

Things settled down in the following century, by which time monastic orders had begun to set up houses within the country, bringing schools, libraries, and other benefits of Western civilization with them. Stephen's family would give 26 saints to the Church, including two Hungarian kings and the queens of a number of other countries, such as the beloved St. Elizabeth of Thuringia and St. Elizabeth of Portugal. The chief role of Hungary was that of buffer for the West against onslaughts from the east: In the 13th century, the great Mongol invasion devastated Hungary and touched Poland briefly but largely spared the West. In the 15th century, the Ottoman Turks moved into Hungarian territory in the Balkans, and in the following century they occupied Hungary for 200 long years of tyranny—with no response from the West.

———————

This role as the outpost of Catholic civilization, absorbing enemy assaults before they could harm the heartland of Europe, was to some extent shared by other Catholic countries of eastern Europe, such as Poland, though Hungary suffered far more from both Mongols and Turks. Following the Turkish conquest, the country came under the rule of the Habsburgs. The 20th century brought worse ills, from the dismemberment of the country

———————

[43] László, p. 145.

by the Allies after World War I to Nazi occupation, which was soon followed by the brutal Communist Russian takeover. In the spiritual life some souls are chosen to suffer as victims for the sins of others in imitation of Christ. There may be nations with analogous vocations. As Cardinal Mindszenty, himself a victim of the last and worst assault on Hungary from the east, by Soviet Russia, put it:

> In defense of civilization, Hungarians have done immortal service that till now has not been rightly honored. Ever since the nation's founding, but especially in the 13th and 14th centuries, their arms kept Western Europe intact. This is why Michelet, in his history of France, calls Hungary the savior of the West. Hungarian blood flowed in streams while Michelangelo quietly conceived the dome of St. Peter's; and while London enjoyed Shakespeare, Hungarians stood guard over the very gates of Rome, London, and Paris. And the reason England has 44, France 41, and Hungary but 10 or 12 million people is that for 500 years Hungary bled for the West, for the world, for civilization.[44]

---

[44] Mindszenty, p. 46.

ℬ Instruments of Conversion ℭ

Education

As Christian civilization grew, education became increasingly important in both evangelization and maintaining the faith in newly converted areas. Charlemagne zealously promoted it, first at his palace and then throughout his empire, in the form of a primary school system for boys and girls. The kind of schooling that had once survived primarily in monasteries and some royal courts was widely promoted by Catholic rulers as an instrument for spreading and strengthening the faith.

By the early Middle Ages urban churches, mainly the larger cathedrals, had begun to organize their own schools with broad curricula. Out of the cathedral schools would come, in turn, the establishment of universities—"corporations" that were independent of local churches and even of the local governments of the cities in which they took root. Education was a crucial instrument of conversion because it was not enough for future apostles to be holy—they had to be able to speak persuasively, they had to be able to read and understand theological and doctrinal material, and they had to possess well-stocked memories and intellectual discipline. Schools, the universities in particular, provided the means to all this through their rigorous courses of study.

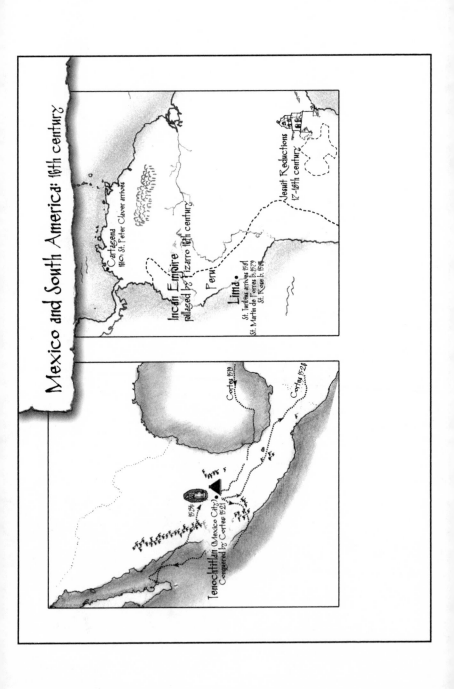

Mexico and South America: 16th century

Cartagena
1610: St. Peter Claver arrives

Incan Empire
pillaged by Pizarro 16th century

Peru

Lima
St. Turibius arrives 1581
St. Martin de Porres b. 1579
St. Rose b. 1586

Jesuit Reductions
17-18th century

Cortez 1519

Cortez 1521

Tenochtitlan (Mexico City)
Conquered by Cortez 1521

1521

5

The Ancient Faith in a New World

We have been examining the origins of the Christian people of the West, which has so far meant Europe. When the colonization of non-Western lands by Europeans began, during the Age of Exploration that opened with the voyages of Columbus in the late 15th century, at least some of those colonies became parts of the West, too. We cannot deal with them all here, but we will examine a few iconic examples of the spread of the faith in the New World: Mexico, Peru, and the region of today's Uruguay and Paraguay.

In earlier chapters we did not consider the conversion of Spain to Christianity because it occurred so early in Christian history and lasted such a short time. Let us look it at briefly here as background to our main topic. The peninsula found itself under Roman rule after the defeat of the North African state of Carthage in the Punic Wars (264-146 B.C.). Carthage had taken over parts of Spain—though not without opposition from the occupied—in the course of expanding its trade network. That ended with the decisive Roman defeat of Carthage, and the Romans, who already had some trading colonies on the peninsula, extended their control over most of Spain. Like the Carthaginians they met with some resistance, but Roman tenacity won out, as it nearly always did, and the country was won over to both Roman government and Roman civilization. It went on to produce some of the great names in Latin literature, such as Quintilian, Seneca, and Martial, along with a few emperors.

Christianity came to Spain sometime in the first century. There is a well-supported tradition that it was brought by St. Paul; there is another tradition that St. James, the patron saint of Spain, also visited the country. This is somewhat problematic, since he is said in Acts 12:1-2 to have been martyred by Herod.

If this occurred in the year 44, as early Christian writers have it, he would not have had much time for Spain. A very old tradition does have our Lady appearing to him in Spain in the year 40, after which he supposedly returned to Jerusalem and was martyred; on the other hand, early Christian writers such as Clement of Alexandria seem to think that he never left Jerusalem after the Ascension. At any rate, Spain certainly adopted Christianity in the century of the apostles, and the Spanish battle cry "For God and St. James!" came to symbolize the nation's old and deep devotion to that son of Zebedee. Like the other provinces of Rome, Spain had its martyrs during the persecutions and produced other saints as well.

A series of barbarian waves hit Spain early in the fifth century as the destructive Vandals passed through on their way to Africa. Other tribes roamed different parts of the country and, amid mutual conflict and the crushing of Catholic resistance, the Visigoths prevailed, with the first Visigothic king in power by 466. Since the Visigoths were Arian, probably converted by those Arians who fled the empire after their condemnation at the Council of Nicaea, that formidable heresy seeped into Spanish religious life. The Catholics did not take it lying down, and there followed a long period of civil war, foreign intervention on one side or the other, the final triumph of the Catholic cause, and, by the early seventh century, the beginning of a fusion of the various ethnic groups into a Spanish identity.

Unfortunately, the end of that century saw the beginning of a period of moral and political decay, and soon after something even worse: the Moorish invasion of the peninsula in 711. Possibly these Moors—the combined forces of Muslim Arabs who had swept across North Africa from Arabia and Berbers from the Atlas region—were invited in by some disgruntled subjects of an unpopular king, but they really needed no invitation: They were out to rule the world.

Moorish Spain soon included all of the country except for a small area in the Asturias Mountains, where the new king,

Pelayo, held out with a number of loyal supporters. That small center of resistance would eventually expand until, in 1492, the last Moorish stronghold of Granada fell to King Ferdinand and Queen Isabella. There was then much to be done, politically and in every other way, to bring Spain to the level of its Christian neighbors with far less turbulent histories. Somehow it was done, and so thoroughly that during the following century Spain became the top power in Europe.

The Beginnings of Empire

It was Isabella who made the fateful decision to support the scheme of Christopher Columbus, who had met with rejection everywhere else he went, to sail to the Far East by going west. Educated people in the 15th century knew the earth was round, so this was not a shocking idea. Nor was the goal unimportant. The growth of Muslim power, particularly after Constantinople fell to the Ottoman Turks, meant that the Muslim conquerors had gained control of what remained of the Eastern Roman Empire in addition to what they already possessed in Arabia, North Africa, Spain, and the Balkans. It also meant that the land route from Europe to Asia was closed to Europeans. For centuries, indeed since Roman times, there had been overland travel by European merchants and others along the Silk Road to China, or by other routes to southern Asian sources of spices and other goods that were much in demand in the West. All that contact was suddenly cut off, and Columbus proposed a way to China that would get around the Turkish obstacle—except that he was to encounter an even bigger obstacle in the form of an enormous land mass that he had not expected, and possibly never really understood. At reviving sea contact between Europe and Asia, Columbus failed; what he did do was open the way for Spanish explorers to acquire a vast new empire that brought for them riches—for Spain new lands and natural resources, and for God, countless immortal souls that had long been under the sway of some of the most diabolic cults known to history.

On his four voyages, Columbus visited the Bahamas, Cuba and other Caribbean islands, and part of the coastline of Central America. Some of those places would soon be settled by Spanish colonists, but for gold, silver, and the other precious things the explorers dreamed of they would have to go further south into the South American continent, and to Mexico—which is what Cortes did. Here we should mention an important point about the mentality of the Spanish, both of the rulers who financed the expeditions and of the explorers themselves. We might presume that greed for wealth and material possessions was the sole motivating force for the Spanish expeditions. Such an explanation seems obvious to the secular, materialistic minds of 21st-century people, who are much like that themselves. The modern mind also abhors the gruesome violence supposedly used by Spanish colonists against nice native people who in their untainted natural virtue were in fact more "civilized" than the brutal Spanish.

The essential element missing here, which the modern secular mind cannot grasp, is that for the Spaniards faith was not the feeble, conventional sectarianism we are used to. They really *believed* that the teachings of the Church alone were true, that Christ meant what he said in telling his followers to make disciples of all nations, that believers would be saved and that those who deliberately refused belief would be condemned. Belief in these doctrines was not limited to Spanish clerics and pious people; it extended to all classes. Thus we will see Cortes, a man of many moral lapses who could hack off a head with the best of them, introducing the subject of religion in his earliest conversations with the Aztec emperor Montezuma and presenting the main points of Christianity to him. The topic was uppermost in his mind, not only for practical reasons—the king told him to convert the pagans, and converted pagans would be easier to deal with—but because he was a believer in the one true faith. Similarly, when the Spaniards realized what went on at the top of the Aztecs' sacred pyramid, they were horrified to the depths of their Catholic souls, and they destroyed, to the extent they could, the paraphernalia of human sacrifice.

With these points in mind, we can now look in some detail at the process of conversion in Spanish America, first in Mexico and then in Central America, with brief excursions south to Peru and Paraguay. Some of the incidents discussed here might recall the satanic powers that St. Patrick faced in Ireland; the details of the incidents are quite different, but the force behind them is the same.

Cortes, Quetzalcoatl, and the Hummingbird Wizard

When Cortes landed in Mexico in 1519 with about 300 men, he had no clear idea of what awaited him except that there was said to be a fabulous and wealthy city somewhere inland ruled by an emperor. As he made his way in the general direction of the city he collected more information from the native tribes he encountered, but nothing prepared him or his men for the reality of what he found. The Aztecs were actually newcomers to the region of Mexico, which had been part of the Toltec empire. The history of the Toltecs is far from clear, though large sculptures and other physical evidence of their culture have been found. They were reputed to have practiced human sacrifice until a beneficent ruler named Quetzalcoatl, named after a feathered-serpent god, stopped the practice. He later dropped out of sight, leaving a legend behind him: he would return in the year 1 Reed, which occurred every 52 years, on the day 1 Wind, coming from the east and wearing black.

Soon after the Spaniards landed in eastern Mexico they were eagerly joined by tens of thousands of native tribesmen who had it in for the Aztecs; one could say that it was actually they who made the "conquest." The question for Cortes was why they were so eager to support him, and he soon found out. The Aztec way of life depended upon human sacrifice. The Aztecs were convinced that their gods required it in order for the weather to be favorable, the fields fertile, and all enterprises successful. Some of the stepped pyramids that dotted the Mexican landscape were used as temples where the human sacrifices were performed. The pyramid in the capital, Tenochtitlan (today's Mexico City), was typical, though likely more elaborate than most. It had a temple at the top with monstrous stone statues of gods, of which the main one was the Hummingbird Wizard; his idol was dressed in various outfits depending on the season, and sometimes decorated with blood and human body parts from the sacrifices. These were performed on a stone table, next to an idol with a gaping mouth. The designated victim would be conducted—or dragged—up the long staircase to where a priest with an obsidian knife was waiting and be bent backwards over the stone slab. Then the priest would deftly cut the heart out of his body and drop it, still pulsing, into the mouth of the idol.

The origin of this ghastly practice has been traced to an influential magician of the previous century who gained great political power because of his influence over the emperor. He insisted on the cult of the Hummingbird Wizard, who thirsted for human blood. In the early days of this cult, the blood donors were probably enemies killed in battle, but the class of victims soon expanded greatly. By the century of Columbus we find a report of 80,000 victims being sacrificed on one single occasion, on the orders of the Hummingbird Wizard, who was said to dictate (through the priestly establishment) the terms of Aztec religious practice, in return giving victory and prosperity to the empire. Reading the accounts of how the system operated leaves the sickening impression of a more than human agency involved here; the "devil gods," as the Spanish called them, were no doubt literally that.

One would suppose that there would be a scarcity of victims, because people would have the sense to flee such a horrible society, or that popular revolt would have put a stop to the appalling practice. One would be wrong. The whole of Aztec society was implicated in this cult, which operated on such a large scale as to make the baby sacrifice of the ancient Carthaginians seem trivial. We do not know to what extent the Aztecs used babies as victims, but they did sacrifice children. Many came from Aztec families that, incredibly, were willing to give them up, possibly considering it an honor for their little boys and girls to be chosen for sacrifices to the god in charge of agricultural fertility. They were kept in nurseries for a short time before their deaths, then taken in procession to the place of execution where their throats were to be slit. People lined the streets as the weeping children were led to their doom and considered their tears to be a good sign of rain to come.

Indeed, there was nothing quiet or hidden about Aztec human sacrifice or the cannibalism that followed it. As historian Inga Clendinnen observed:

> The killings were not remote top-of-the-pyramid affairs. If only the high priests and rulers killed, they carried out most of their butchers' work *en plein air*, and not only in the temple precinct, but in the neighbourhood temples and on the streets. The people were implicated in the care and preparation of the victims, their delivery to the place of death, and then in the elaborate processing of the bodies: the dismemberment and distribution of heads and limbs, flesh and blood and flayed skins. On high occasions warriors carrying gourds of human blood or wearing the dripping skins of their captives ran through the streets, to be ceremoniously welcomed into the dwellings; the flesh of their victims seethed in domestic cooking pots; human thighbones, scraped and dried, were set up in the courtyards of the households—and all this among a people notable for a precisely ordered polity, a grave formality of manner, and a developed regard for beauty.[45]

The Aztecs did use slaves for sacrifices, but their main supply of victims seems to have come from ritual "flower wars" they fought against neighboring tribes. Here we come to the main reason they were so hated by their neighbors. The wars of the

---

[45] Windschuttle, p. 68, quoting Clendinnen, *Aztecs: An Interpretation* (Cambridge: Cambridge University Press, 1991) p. 2.

Aztecs generally had no motive except that of obtaining captives to be sacrificed; hence, they did not kill in battle (the Spaniards would be puzzled by this) but concentrated on taking prisoners. The fate of the prisoners was never in doubt.

That is why tens of thousands of Indians, each of them a potential oblation to the Hummingbird Wizard, joined the Spaniards on their way to the capital of the Aztec empire. This trip took many months and was described in great detail by Bernal Diaz del Castillo, Cortes's secretary and invaluable eyewitness to many events. Everywhere they stopped, the Spaniards arranged an altar on which their priests said Mass, setting upon it "the sacred image of our Lady and the Cross."[46] This reference to an image of our Lady is found frequently in Diaz's diary, illustrating the prominent place the Spaniards gave to the Queen of Heaven. They would greatly need her help when, following the conquest, they found widespread resistance to conversion among the Indians. Secretly, perhaps, the Hummingbird Wizard was still at work then, producing alienation between conquered and conquerors, no matter how many benefits the Spanish lavished on their new colony and its people. More than human effort was needed for the conversion of Mexico, and so our Lady in person took up the task, as we will see. Meanwhile, we must observe the harrowing course of events—harrowing for both conquered and conquerors—that led up to that divine intervention.

Montezuma's Dilemma

Emperor Montezuma heard of the strangers' approach and apparently was unsure of how to react. It seems the year (1519) happened to be 1 Reed, the day happened to be 1 Wind, Cortes was certainly coming from the east, and because it was Good Friday he was wearing black. Could he be Quetzalcoatl returning? Thus the first contacts were peaceful, though the Spanish had been preceded by stories of the monstrous animals on which

---

[46] Diaz, p. 64.

they rode and of their noisy metal rods that could kill. Through interpreters, Cortes and Montezuma exchanged presents and courtesies, and Cortes mentioned that he had been sent by a great emperor "to see him, and to beg them to become Christians the same as our emperor and all of us, so that his soul and those of all his vassals might be saved."[47]

Gradually, during those first peaceful days, he explained to Montezuma the main tenets of the faith. When the emperor remarked that he had heard reports of crosses set up by his guests, Cortes replied that the gods of the Aztecs were devils, but that they dared not come to the places where the crosses were; he also said that soon some men would come who led very holy lives, much better than the soldiers did, and who would explain their religion to the Indians. Here Montezuma answered, "I have understood your words and arguments very well . . . about the three gods and the cross. . . . We have not made any answer to it because here throughout all time we have worshiped our own gods, and thought they were good, as no doubt yours are, so do not trouble to speak to us any more about them at present."[48] In all these early exchanges, Montezuma comes across as a mild-mannered man, fond of laughter and courteous conversation and willing to do everything to make his guests comfortable. Still, he is known to have worshiped the Hummingbird Wizard and to have ordered and witnessed human sacrifices as a matter of course. His polite dismissal of the topic of religion prefigures the resistance that would prevail among the Aztecs for another decade.

Although the emperor might remain well disposed to his new European friends, it was not so with the priestly establishment whose influence over him was so great. It seems that most of the Spaniards did not realize the horrifying practices that were going on not far from the comfortable palace where they were lodged, though Diaz observed Cortes—who may have

[47] Diaz, p. 204.
[48] Ibid.

suspected—passing up the meat course during a banquet. Cortes and his men were impressed with the architecture of the city, the fabulous marketplace—said by the most traveled among them to be more wonderful than anything in Europe or Byzantium—and the great zoo. (The latter provided for convenient disposal of leftover body parts from the sacrifices.)

When Cortes realized the truth about the human sacrifices, he took Montezuma prisoner and commanded him to order the cessation of the practice. This was done, but it alienated the Aztec population, particularly the priestly caste. When in 1520 Cortes had to leave Tenochtitlan temporarily, a fight broke out in June between Spanish and Aztecs, and when he returned to an out-of-control situation the battle was joined in earnest. In the course of the fighting, a stone apparently thrown by an Aztec killed Montezuma—one of his nephews was implicated—perhaps accidentally, perhaps in retaliation for his stopping of the sacrifices. Now the Spanish conquest began in earnest.

Historians debate the question of how a small number of Spaniards in an unfamiliar land could have defeated the great Aztec empire, even with the support of their Indian allies in some engagements. Without going into details of the whole campaign, we note that the Spaniards were first forced to leave—indeed, flee—the capital because of the number of causalities they were sustaining as well as their fatigue and lack of provisions. They managed to make it out of the city and sought refuge with a friendly tribe. Other Spanish soldiers from the Atlantic coast joined them, but many of Cortes's force, both men and horses, were in such poor condition that several advisors argued for abandoning the idea of returning to Tenochtitlan.

Cortes, however, was adamant. The city was partially built on islands in a lake, and he spent time assembling a small fleet of boats and planning for the siege and land assault. In the fall of 1520, smallpox devastated the Aztec population in the capital; the bacillus had been unknowingly brought to America by the Spanish, who were unaffected by it. In early 1521, Cortes began placing groups of his men around the city in preparation for the final siege; the actual fighting on the outskirts began in May and the main battle within the city took place during June and July.

This final and decisive attack on the city was tragic and costly. Time and time again the Aztecs refused offers of negotiation, and the fighting went wearily on. The soldiers had witnessed the capture and gruesome sacrifice of many of their friends and allies, which stiffened their determination to conquer. When the fighting finally tipped decisively in their favor, the Spaniards charged up the pyramid, the fanatical priests of the Hummingbird Wizard fighting them at every step, and destroyed everything they could. The Spanish soon found that as long as the Aztecs were capable of fighting there was no way of eliciting surrender from them because they believed that their enemies would surely do to them what they did to their own prisoners. This tragic misapprehension, along with profound differences in military maneuvers between the two sides, led to the unnecessary deaths of numerous Aztec warriors. Spanish casualties, on the other hand, included soldiers who were captured and sacrificed in a temple, their severed heads brought back to the battlefield and shown to their comrades. Cortes himself survived several moments in the final battle when he could easily have been slain; the Aztecs believed that an enemy leader must not be killed in battle but taken captive and sacrificed, and the warriors who managed to get close to Cortes seem to have quarreled over who was to get the credit for taking him, allowing him to escape. At length, on August 13, 1521, after a 93-day siege, the ruling emperor was captured and it was all over. The Indian allies took appalling revenge on their longtime enemies. They killed not only the Aztec warriors but the children, so they could never grow up to fight, and the elders, so they could not pass on the military traditions of the empire.

The empire was defeated, though it would take decades for Spanish administration to encompass it all—a large area populated by Aztecs and other tribes that stretched north, south, east, and west from Tenochtitlan. In some towns and cities, the arrival of Spanish forces elicited revolts, which had to be put down; sometimes the repression was harsh, which resulted in hostility toward the Spanish and lack of openness to European culture, including Christianity.

After the Conquest, a New Mexico

Cortes, though, proved to be an enlightened conqueror. Over the next few years, he made grants of land to his own men but also to prominent Aztecs. Self-governing native towns were set up in which Spaniards were neither to live nor to work. The Indians governed themselves using their native language (Nahuatl) and were required only to pay taxes and allow missionaries to visit them. Except for a small number of prisoners of war, Cortes allowed no slavery, and King Philip III later abolished all Indian personal servitude and employment on sugar plantations. By 1539, the pope had excommunicated anyone guilty of enslaving or robbing the Indians. We might pause here to consider whether any previous conquest in history proceeded thusly, or whether the English and Americans behaved similarly in their later conquests of the North American Indians. (To raise the question is to answer it.)

There were abuses, of course, though nothing on the scale alleged by the enemies of Spain. Some Spaniards treated the Indians under their control as slaves, and when silver mines were discovered, the Indians were made to labor there in harsh conditions; some of the successors of Cortes were unusually cruel and greedy in governing; the king of Spain, who was concerned with the promotion of both the faith and of justice in his new colony, was far away. (Much of the difficulty in dealing with abuses in the colonies—all colonies of any nation—stemmed from the length of time needed for communication with governmental authorities in the mother country.) To deal with this problem, the king appointed the bishop of Mexico as "Protector of the Indians," and the first holder of that title smuggled evidence against the local governor back to Spain in a sailor's pack where no one would think to look for it: It was hidden in a slab of bacon that was in turn placed in a vat of oil. It is hard to imagine that the papers were legible (or what they smelled like) when they got to the king, but apparently they were, and the governor was replaced. Pope Paul III was concerned with affairs in Mexico, and in 1537 he declared that the Indians should not "be treated like irrational animals and used exclusively for our profit and our service. . . . [They] must not be deprived of their freedom and their possessions . . . even if they are not Christians, and on the contrary, they must be left to enjoy their freedom and their possessions." He emphasized the Christian principle that "every person is my brother or sister."[49]

Under Cortes, the first hospital for Indians was established, and by 1534 there would be schools for Indian girls. In 1539 the first printing press in the New World was set up, printing translations of all sorts for the Indians. Orphanages, trade schools, and colleges followed, and even a university for Aztec students, founded in 1551. The curriculum was modeled on that of Salamanca, and the Aztecs proved to be diligent learners. When the first class graduated, the Spanish tried to turn the school over to them, to run it for their own people. This seems to have been less than successful; the Indians might be brilliant students, but at that point they still lacked management and organizational skills. (Those skills would come, however, to the point that a full-blooded descendent of Montezuma was later appointed viceroy of Mexico by the Spanish king. Racist the Spanish were not.)

In the first years following the conquest, conversion of the Aztecs and other Mexican tribes proceeded slowly, despite the best efforts of dedicated Franciscan missionaries. Particularly in areas where there was little governmental presence, relations between Spanish colonists and the Indians were often strained, and this evidently hindered the natives' receptivity to the religion of

---

[49] Hanke, pp. 72-73.

the white man. In 1531 this all changed, thanks to the mysterious appearance of the image of a young woman—clearly the Virgin Mary—on the cloak of a middle-aged Aztec man.

This man, Juan Diego, thought that what he held in his cloak was a bundle of flowers, placed there by a young woman who had appeared to him a number of times in the desert outside Mexico City, asking that the bishop build a church to her. When Juan Diego, after much hassle, came into the presence of the bishop and allowed his rolled-up cloak to fall open, he was startled to see all those present kneel down in veneration: they saw not only flowers, but also the extraordinary image now known as the *tilma* of our Lady of Guadalupe.[50] Scientific analysis has not revealed any human means by which the image could have been produced. It was not painted (although it has been touched up with paint over the centuries); the cloth should have disintegrated within a generation but is still in perfect condition over four centuries after it was first woven; high magnification shows figures in the eyes of the image—apparently those reflected in the living eyes of our Lady at the moment when Juan Diego unfolded his cloak; and these are only some of the features of this celebrated relic. Most singularly, the image depicts a pregnant

---

[50] Here we must ask why the name of a Marian shrine in Spain, Guadalupe, has come to denote this Mexican image. The word apparently first occurs in Juan Diego's report of what his sick uncle told him. It was as he was hurrying to fetch help for the ailing man that our Lady appeared to Juan Diego, but he later learned from his uncle that she had appeared to him too, leaving him cured and referring to herself as "Holy Mary of Guadalupe." Since the Aztec language lacks the letters *g* and *d*, it has been argued that the word used could not have been that. Warren Carroll points out, however, in his book *Our Lady of Guadalupe and the Conquest of Darkness*, that the words of both Juan Diego and his uncle were relayed to the bishop and other Spaniards through a trained interpreter who would not have mistaken a Nahuatl term for a Spanish one. Mary must actually have used the word *Guadalupe*, possibly to connect the traditional veneration of her in Guadalupe in Spain with that which would develop in New Spain.

Aztec woman and contains symbols that conveyed a spiritual meaning to the Aztecs. From the time it first appeared, miracles were associated with it, and within six years there was a mass conversion of some 9 million Aztecs. As Warren Carroll puts it, "It should be self-evident that this immense surge of baptisms beginning in 1532—these millions of Indians suddenly seeking out the sacrament of Christian initiation with an overwhelming desire, *even when not yet in contact with the missionaries, where most of them had previously held back despite the best efforts of the missionaries* and the prestige of the conquerors—derives primarily from the impact of the apparition and the portrait."[51]

This is an extremely interesting point on which to reflect; millions of Indians had refused conversion "despite the best efforts of the missionaries," but here were multitudes asking for baptism who had not yet even met any missionaries! The only possible explanation for this phenomenon is a supernatural one: the Mediatrix of All Graces poured out graces in such strength and abundance that they moved the most obdurate souls—a miracle on a par with the miracle of the apparition itself. Where even faithful, courageous, and diligent human effort had mostly failed, the extraordinary grace of God's providence succeeded.

The consequences of this mass conversion cannot be over-emphasized. Conquered and conquerors now shared a common religion; since the Spanish were not racially prejudiced, as the English were, they were now willing to intermarry with the natives, which eventually produced a racially and religiously homogenous society. The power of the devil gods—at least in Mexico—was destroyed by the Woman who crushed the head of the Serpent.

––––––––––

Eventually Spain (along with Portugal) would control the entire South American continent, which was inhabited by a great

––––––––––

[51] Hanke, p. 109 (italics mine).

variety of tribes with disparate civilizations or, in some cases, a total lack of civilization. As soon as the conquest of Mexico became known, explorers and soldiers of fortune from Spain and elsewhere in Europe began pushing into the uncharted areas of Central and South America in search of precious metals and productive land. When within a few years, most of the continent was in Spanish or Portuguese hands, and the situation in the new colonies was quite different from that which we saw in Mexico. Cortes brought many priests and monks on his expedition, with the conversion of the natives high on his list of goals, but this was not the case with the treasure-seekers who vied for control of the southern continent. On their expeditions there was sometimes a token priest to attend to the members' spiritual needs, sometimes none at all. They cared not about the natives' souls but their land and their gold. Yet, as we shall see, some of the peoples who were brutally treated by their rapacious overlords became the most zealous converts and produced great saints.

We will look at two vastly different regions that would end up under Spanish rule. The first is the empire of the Incas, conquered by the conquistador Pizarro and his cronies. I recall the late Warren Carroll remarking that comparing Cortes and Pizarro is like comparing Churchill and Stalin; we will not expect much in the way of Catholic virtue or even intelligence from Pizarro.

The Inca Imperium and Its Conversion

From a small tribal unit in the 12th century to a sort of city-state organization in the 13th, the Incas developed and expanded their territories until, by the time the Spanish learned of them, they controlled a large empire, with its capital at Cuzco, that included much of western South America. Civilization is said to be distinguished from barbarism by the two marks of urban life and a written language. The Incas are counted as a civilized people for three centuries of their history (14th to 16th centuries); they did have urban settlements, but they did not know writing. Thus there is much that we do not know about them and their history. They depended on the equivalent of bards to pass on the record of events orally and on other memory specialists to transmit the meaning of mathematical symbols. Their architecture shows fine craftsmanship, and they possessed large quantities of gold, which they used for decoration rather than for coinage. They worshiped nature gods and practiced human sacrifice, usually of young children. The children would be taken to high altitudes, given intoxicating or hallucinogenic beverages, and then either left to die of exposure or suffocated as offerings to the gods. Whether the Incas also practiced cannibalism is unclear.

Francisco Pizarro, his brothers, and some other adventurers who had sailed west eager for land and plunder encountered the Incas in the early 16th century and were soon engaged in subjugating the empire and its many resources. The tale of this conquest is a sordid one, marked by abuse and forced labor of the Incas, civil war and murders among groups of conquistadors, and even revolt against the authority of the Spanish crown when the king forbade forced Indian labor. The contrast between Cortes, with his genuine desire to avoid bloodshed and to bring the Aztecs to Christ, and Pizarro and his men ("ruthless plunderers and killers," according to Carroll[52]) could hardly be greater. Pizarro's treatment of the Inca emperor Atahualpa illustrates this. At the first meeting between the Spanish and the emperor, the day after the conquistadors' arrival in 1533, what had promised to be a peaceful outdoor get-together became a scene of slaughter when Pizarro suddenly and loudly ordered his men to charge (regrettably using the Spanish battle cry, *"Santiago,"* thereby calling on St. James to help the invaders commit an atrocity). The emperor was seized, and several thousand unarmed spectators in the plaza were cut down with Spanish swords. The following day, Pizarro told the emperor that he would be released if he would order the room in which he was being held to be filled with gold to

---

[52] Carroll, *The Cleaving of Christendom*, p. 155.

a certain height. This was done. Pizarro seized the gold and had the emperor killed anyway.

Pizarro had brought only one token priest with him, the Dominican Vincent de Valverde. It was he who, through an interpreter, had attempted to explain Christianity to the emperor when they first met. By some accounts, the Inca had been given some holy object and thrown it to the ground, whereupon Father de Valverde instigated the Spanish attack. Other sources dispute this as a calumny, and it does seem that during his imprisonment Atahualpa received instructions from the priest and was baptized before his death. The rest of Valverde's career, until his murder by Indians while he was on his way to Panama, is highly controversial. It included his appointment as the first bishop of Cuzco and to the office of Protector of the Indians, but some contemporary accounts accuse him of treating Indians badly and even keeping some of them as slaves. Those charges may be falsehoods leveled for political reasons; nonetheless, a saint, it seems, he was not.

When the Spaniards had completed the conquest of Peru and order was at last restored, a large group of Franciscans came to Lima, where they set up schools and hospitals, but the continuing ill treatment of the natives by the ruthless Spaniards interfered with progress in conversion. In the 1560s, the Jesuits began to arrive and soon produced a bilingual catechism (the first book published in South America). Conversions began to pick up, though still at a slow pace. Then came a divine surprise in the form of an unlikely bishop who was also a saint. Toribio Alfonso de Mogrovejo was a nobleman and a law professor at Salamanca University. King Philip II knew of his many talents and decided to appoint him archbishop of Peru—despite the fact that he was then a layman. In 1578 he was ordained, consecrated two years later, and shipped off to Peru, where he landed in 1581, some six hundred miles from Lima. From there he proceeded to walk to his episcopal seat, preaching, teaching, and baptizing as he went. As bishop he continued this practice, three times during the course of his career visiting all the parts of his 18,000-square-mile archdiocese almost entirely on foot.

It is hard to find a good work that St. Turibius (as we know him) did not perform. He built roads, chapels, churches, schools, hospitals, convents, and the first American seminary, at Lima, in 1591. He called synods and councils to improve oversight of the vast area under his care. To say that he made a difference in the bleak conversion record of the Spanish in South America is an understatement. It is estimated that he baptized and confirmed nearly half a million people, among them three saints: Rose of Lima, Martin de Porres, and Francis Solano. When he died in 1606 (on the day that one tradition says had been revealed to him years before), the conversion of South America had been greatly advanced.

Converting the Overlooked: The Guarani

So far in this chapter we have dealt with the conversion of civilized, even advanced tribes—however unpleasant their civilizations. Now there are two very different groups that deserve our attention: the natives of the Central American jungle who still lived essentially in the Stone Age, and the African slaves who, beginning in the 16th century, were brought in large numbers to Spanish America.

To take the Stone Agers first, we must go to the borderlands between Uruguay and Paraguay, where the Guarani lived a hunter-gatherer lifestyle, wary of contact with Europeans. In that no-man's land without cultivation or much governmental oversight, slave traders lay in wait for natives to capture and outlaws to steal whatever they could. Thus the Jesuits found it hard to establish relations with the Guarani until they hit upon a common love of music; it turned out that the Guarani not only responded to the missionaries singing and playing on simple instruments, but they had a great gift for music themselves. Once contact was established and conversions began, by the early 17th century the Jesuits began to set up unique settlements ("reductions") for their charges in remote areas away from rapacious settlers. They taught the Guarani skills, crafts, and agricultural techniques as well as religion, and the natives themselves were soon building their own churches, fortifications, storehouses, and workshops. They learned techniques of self-government and law enforcement, together with reading, writing, and other basic skills. They made their own musical instruments, copying European models, and loved to perform and sing at Masses and festivals.

The reductions were a bold enterprise for the 17th century, and as they spread they made a number of enemies. Slave traders were robbed of their prey; neighboring tribes envied Guarani prosperity and sometimes attacked and looted settlements. Enemies of the Jesuits (and they were many, from envious members of other orders and suspicious Spanish officials to the Archenemy of all good) complained that they were setting up little private kingdoms that interfered with governmental organization and taxation. They were becoming too powerful, and who knew what they might not do with an army raised from the reductions? Anti-Jesuit sentiment and European politics forced the suppression of the order and its expulsion from Spanish territories in 1767. Without their directors, the Guarani could not hold on to their little oases of faith, tranquility, and civilization. Preyed upon by their many enemies, they slowly dispersed into larger society or melted back into the jungle in the course of the following century. Travelers who met some of them in later times were told tales of a golden age when they had lived in prosperous and peaceful communities built around their churches and their beloved fathers.

Converting the Invisible: African Slaves

The problem African slavery posed to the Church and her missionaries differed in many respects from the difficulty of reaching the souls of the South American Indians. Ironically, the demand for African slave labor was partially due to the condemnation, by both the Church and the Spanish government, of Indian slavery.

Also, enslaved Indians forced to work in the mines and on agricultural plantations were unsuited to such work and died in large numbers; it was thought, or at least hoped, that African laborers would be more hardy. As a result, many hundreds of thousands of slaves began pouring into the seaport of Cartagena to be sold at auction there or transported further inland. Conditions on the slave ships were appalling; the miserable creatures, stolen from their homes by slave-traders and sold to African slave merchants, were chained together in overcrowded, fetid, dark holds—the dead and dying yoked to the living throughout the long voyage of several months. It was said that no white man could go down into the hold and live, the stench was so poisonous.

In Cartagena there was a Jesuit house to which a young novice from Spain named Peter Claver was sent in 1610. His mentor was Father Alonso de Sandoval, who has been called the first abolitionist. Sandoval had worked for decades with the newly arrived Africans, learning their languages, asking them about their former homes, customs, foods, and other details which he used to write a pioneering work in African ethnography, which is sometimes called the first abolitionist work. He wanted to know all about the backgrounds and diets of the slaves so that he could provide them with suitable care. Peter Claver, who considered himself "the slave of the slaves," continued in the footsteps of Father Sandoval. For 40 years he met every slave ship that came into Cartagena, first going down into the holds to tend to the most urgent needs of the prisoners, bringing lemons because so many suffered from scurvy, then following up on those first contacts. He had a garden in which he grew some of the vegetables familiar to West Africans, and he made periodic visits to farms to check on the living conditions there.

As part of the Jesuit community in Cartagena, St. Peter was known and respected by the Spanish community, though some may have thought him a little too protective of "his" slaves and resented his watchfulness over them. With the help of a small group of interpreters whom he made catechists, he taught the faith to the slaves, baptized them, and welcomed them to the church where he preached and heard confessions. (With some regularity, it seems: One Spanish lady complained to him that she had to stand in line for confession behind slaves.) Unpopular as his work and methods were, he got away with everything; he was, after all, known as a miracle-worker and prophet and performed severe penances in addition to his exhausting activities. It is estimated that out of the million slaves that passed through Cartagena, St. Peter had contact with at least three hundred thousand. After 40 years of this missionary work, the slave trade dried up at Cartagena (though not everywhere in Spanish America), so Peter began making plans to go to West Africa and help his beloved Africans in their homeland. He died before his dream was realized but left, along with Father Sandoval and the other Jesuits who labored for justice and salvation for the slaves, an example of holiness and great charity.

It is impossible to calculate the number of converts made in the Americas by the Spaniards, particularly by the saints among them, not to mention those converted by our Lady herself. Could there have been still more had there been more representatives of the Spanish crown like Cortes and fewer like Pizarro? Probably. Nevertheless, the planting of the faith throughout the vast lands of Spanish America was a great achievement, all the more impressive when we reflect that virtually all the tribes converted remained Catholic, at least to some degree, throughout the centuries.

Catholic principles informed Hispanic society in numerous ways. Because they were not racist, the Catholic Spanish intermarried with both Catholic Indians and Catholic Africans. Although slavery persisted for some time in the Spanish colonies, there were major differences between the system there and in Protestant North America: In Spanish America, slave marriages were considered true marriages and spouses could not be sold away from each other or from their children, as they could in the American South; a slave could marry the wife he chose, even one of another race; he could go to court to be freed from an cruel master. These were a few of the provisions that made the institution, evil as it was, far less cruel than the plantation system the English inflicted on their slaves in North America. Millions of Indians in the Spanish and Portuguese possessions converted to the true faith. Despite individual instances of cruel massacres by fiends like Pizarro, they were not annihilated or forced onto reservations like most North American tribes. One can only speculate what the course of history would have been had the colonizers of North America been Catholic, not Protestant (and especially not Puritan) and been accompanied to the New World by missionaries—including saints, as God graciously provided to the South American settlers. The whole destiny of the North American Indians and slaves, and probably of the world, would have been quite different from what it has been.

Finally, the conversion story of Spanish America presents the most spectacular intervention of heaven that we find in any missionary undertaking. We have seen many miracles in the course of the events surveyed in this book, but nothing as wonderful as those surrounding the appearance of our Lady's portrait, which continues to be a powerful means of grace for the Americas, both North and South. As she told Juan Diego, she is the mother of "all who dwell in these lands."

❧ INSTRUMENTS OF CONVERSION ☙

DIVINE INTERVENTION

Throughout the sacred history recounted in the Old Testament, we often see the direct intervention of God in human affairs, and this intervention is also present in the New Testament, even after the Ascension of our Lord. St. Paul's conversion and St. Philip's disappearance and heavenly transportation to another place, following his conversation with the Ethiopian eunuch, are two such examples (Acts 8). In post-biblical times such direct intervention became more rare, though miracles performed by saints, as well as heavenly apparitions, still occurred, greatly supporting the work of conversion.

Indeed, in all these cases, God intervened in extraordinary ways to convert souls: Paul's, the eunuch's, and those of the millions of Indians within the Aztec empire and the rest of the Americas. Such heavenly activity as a unique conversion instrument: rare, unexpected, and spectacularly effective.

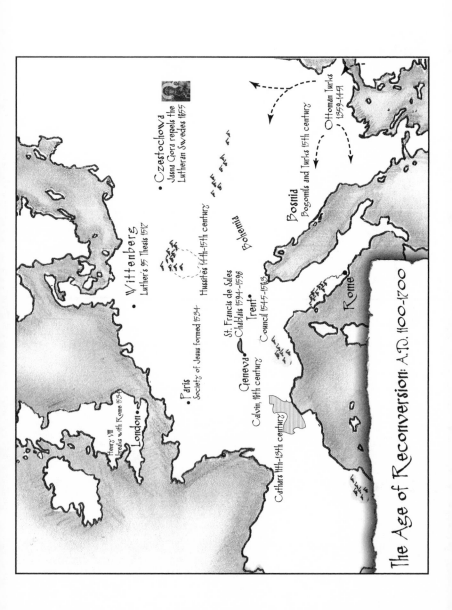

The Age of Reconversion: A.D. 1100–1700

Cathars 11th–13th century

Calvin, 16th century

Geneva

St. Francis de Sales
Chablais 1594–1598

Trent•
Council 1545–1563

Paris•
Society of Jesus formed 1534

London•

Henry VIII
breaks with Rome 1534

• Wittenberg
Luther's 95 Theses 1517

Hussites 14th–15th century

Bohemia

• Czestochowa
Jasna Gora repels the
Lutheran Swedes 1655

Bosnia
Bogomils and Turks 15th century

Ottoman Turks
1359–1453

Rome•

6

Rebellion and Reconversion

Here it would be nice to sum up the successful conversions we have been following and rejoice in all the happy endings. The Romans, Celts, Franks, Goths, Slavs, Magyars, and Spanish Indians have entered the bosom of the Church, never to leave that blessed fold of the Good Shepherd. Or have they? Unfortunately, converted peoples who have turned to the Church can also turn against her, some never to return. Some of the peoples whose conversions we have traced went back (in whole or in part) to paganism, while others re-embraced old heresies or adopted new ones. In short, the story is never finished because all those souls needed, or still need, to be re-evangelized, to be converted anew. Hence our final topic: the problem of reconversion.

In one sense, reconversion is a constant in the Christian life. We must continually renew or revive our faith and the virtues connected with it, sometimes daily. More precisely, though, the term *reconversion* refers to the bringing back to assent to the doctrines of the faith those who had professed them once and then rejected them. In the last chapter we noted this problem briefly in connection with the Catholics who became Arian in Visigothic Spain. Unlike most of the Arian tribes of the Dark Ages, who went from paganism to the heretical Christianity of Arius, those Spaniards lapsed into it from the true religion they had received.

The work of reconversion is different, and probably harder, than converting unbelievers for the first time. With pagans, Christian missionaries always tried to find some common ground on which to base their discussions. We see St. Paul trying this in his address on the Areopagus in Athens; looking at all the temples around him he told his listeners that he could tell they were "very religious." He did not start out by attacking their temple worship but by admiring their religious sentiment. It did not go over well with the sophisticated Greek intellectuals, but that was only one instance. As Cardinal Newman writes in discussing the fourth-century Church of Alexandria, the way to deal with pagans was first to ask them about their beliefs and then praise those that could be praised. He states that all religious knowledge comes in some way from God and that "there is something true and divinely revealed, in every religion all over the earth, overloaded as it may be, and at times even stifled by the impieties which the corrupt will and understanding of man have incorporated with it."[53] He goes so far as to claim that "Job was a pagan in the same sense in which the Eastern nations are pagans in the present day. He lived among idolaters, yet he and his friends had cleared themselves from the superstitions with which the true creed was beset."[54] He cites other Old Testament examples of elements of divine truth and inspiration among the pagans. Building on the positive elements present in most pagan cults, Christians could gradually induce cult adherents to consider Catholic truths that were in harmony with those elements. We have seen Cortes trying to do this in his early conversations with Montezuma, for instance; it is a tried and true tactic of successful missionaries in all ages.

Most of the pagans converted during the Dark Ages remained for a long time within the Church. The majority of the Poles and Irish, for example, never left (except in the northern part of Ireland, where the English planted a Protestant colony), despite attempts by Reformation preachers to draw them into heresy. In later centuries, however, heresies and schisms arose in nearly all the nations of Europe. Although Spanish America was largely spared the devastation caused in Europe by the Reformation and the heresies that preceded it, the early 20th century saw the rise of militant Freemasonry in Mexico—which made

---

[53] Newman, p. 80.

[54] Ibid., p. 81.

martyrs of many Mexican Catholics—and by the end of the century numerous sects and cults had begun poaching Catholic souls throughout the southern continent. The problem for the Church then became how to bring *back* the souls of those who had once welcomed the faith but were now adherents of false doctrines. This was a more complex issue than converting pagans who were merely ignorant of Christianity.

As Newman puts it, "Origen and others were not unwilling to be on a footing of intercourse with the heathen philosophers of their day, in order, if it were possible, to lead them to the truth; but deliberate heretics and apostates, those who had known the truth, and rejected it, were objects of their abhorrence, and were avoided from the truest charity to them. For what can be said to those who already know all that we have to say?"[55] Many of those who went into heresy knew well what they were rejecting; were they then to be simply avoided, as Origen and Newman advised? In some cases, that was probably the only reasonable course to pursue. Still, there were many apostates who had become such mainly through ignorance; they had never been properly taught the truths of the faith or were never well instructed in how to live it. Then there were those who had never cared enough to learn about their religion in the first place. When something new came along that promised material or social advantages, they joined it willingly. The ignorant and the apathetic were easy prey for heretics who professed to be more holy and learned than the local Catholic priests.

Historically, the biggest threat to Catholicism in the West, and the greatest challenge to reconversion, was the Reformation. But even before and after it, other attempts were made—and are, of course, still being made—to wrest souls from the Church. Accordingly, in each case the Church expended great effort to wrest them back—its champions showing no less courage and cunning than the martyrs of Rome or the Jesuits of the jungle.

---

[55] Ibid., p. 86.

Arianism Redux

We recall that the heresy of Arius, disentangled from the elegant verbiage in which it was framed, was simply that Christ is not God. He is God's first creature and creates the rest of creation but is not himself divine. Political and cultural elements complicated the issue, with many Greek-speaking intellectuals in the Eastern Roman Empire supporting one of their own, Emperor Constantine first supporting and then condemning the Arians, and those whose main goal was to be on the right side of the ruler lurching from one position to another. Those most involved in the theological struggle, like poor St. Athanasius, were repeatedly exiled, then recalled, then banished again.

Arian intellectuals certainly fit Newman's category of "those who already know all that we have to say." In case they had missed something, their Catholic opponents cited scriptural passages that clearly contradicted the central Arian premise, including our Lord's own statement, "I and the Father are one" (John 10:30) and "In the beginning was the Word, and the Word was with God, and the Word was God" (John 1:1), as well as other passages from the Gospels and St. Paul's letters. There were also theological arguments to be made: If Christ was not both God and man, how could he have redeemed mankind? There were philosophical arguments, based on the concepts of being and essence. Finally, when all that could be done by the theologians had been done without effect, there was the infallible authority of the Catholic Church, which declared dogmatically, in the ecumenical Council of Nicaea, that Arianism was false and that Christ is "consubstantial with the Father."

Finally defeated and condemned, the Arian exiles took their heresy to the barbarians.

This created a different challenge for Catholic apologists, who had the unenviable task of telling the Arian barbarians that they had been wrong twice: first in having been pagans and then in accepting a heretical gospel. The uneducated Vandals, Visigoths, and Germanic tribes would not have understood the essential theological and philosophical arguments. For them, their new religion was a cultural thing. It was part of their tribal identity and distinguished them from their Catholic, Roman foes. They had their own barbarian rituals, held under the moon in the woods, and were proud of their creed, whether they understood it or not.

As with most barbarian groups, they followed their rulers in religion as in everything else. If a powerful tribal chief became an Arian, his people were likely to follow him. (We recall that the conversion of Clovis to Catholicism was followed by mass conversions of his Franks.) It is for this reason that missionaries to the barbarians tried first to convert rulers and their families, realizing the great influence a chief's religion would exercise on his followers and the power of example that Catholic wives and husbands could give their Arian (or pagan, as in the case of Clovis) spouses. Converted Catholic chiefs were also a great asset to the missionaries' efforts, building churches, endowing monasteries, and conformeding their laws to Christian principles.

Over generations, Arianism as a social force disappeared from Europe. The ruling classes were converted (or reconverted) to the faith and instituted a Catholic political order, and members of formerly Arian families were weaned away from their heresy by intermarriage with Catholics and by exposure to Catholic teaching and missionary activity. Though the spread of Catholic education reinforced solid doctrinal knowledge among ordinary Catholics, making it harder for Arianism to survive, its basic doctrines would not completely die out. Its familiar christological errors would reappear in various minor European heresies and indeed persist in present-day sects such as the Jehovah's Witnesses and Unitarians. It is possible that some of the appeal of later Protestant sects stemmed from the manner in which they recalled to German converts their ancient religion, which was identified in their eyes as a German thing. False doctrines die hard.

Medieval Heresies

Because Satan never quits, all through the Middle Ages we find heterodox groups popping up and infecting parts of Catholic Europe. Some were primarily reactions to moral failings of the clergy, some were bound up with questions of political authority, and others adopted bizarre doctrines that had filtered in from outlying areas, such as the Balkans.

In 11th-century Florence, for example, we find militant crusaders for clerical reform, probably part of the Milanese movement called the *Pataria*, protesting at the house of a priest who did not fit their standards of behavior. At some point, they decided to say it with brickbats and hatchets and attacked the priest's house, enforcing clerical poverty by stealing what was in it. Whatever their motivation or the ideas espoused by these disaffected people, the problem of dissident sects that resorted to violence concerned both Church and state. Everywhere in the West political harmony depended to a large extent upon religious harmony; the king was God's representative in secular matters as the pope was in spiritual things. Heresy, especially in its more disorderly manifestations, was thus considered an affront to social, religious, and political order, and was censured by both Church and state.

Thus we find the Emperor Frederick II (one of the Awful People of history, though that is another story) eliminating heresy in his 13th-century territories by eliminating the heretics—in gruesome ways. He cared little for orthodoxy except to the extent that it made his subjects more docile; heresy was a merely political nuisance to him (he would become a heretic himself). The Church took the position that heresy must be eliminated, but by the conversion—not the death—of the heretic. Only in the case of serious resistance, when persuasion failed and the presence of determined heretics became a clear danger to souls, did the Church resort to calling for the banishment of the troublemakers. (The Latin verb *exterminare*, meaning to put someone outside the borders of a territory, has sometimes been deliberately mistranslated to indicate an intention to incinerate the poor wretches.) As heretical sects developed during the Middle Ages, particularly in times of economic or political breakdown, the need arose for a methodical means of investigating and dealing with the problem.

The Inquisition

Suppressing the obligatory shudder that the term supposedly requires, we will look at the Inquisition's role in reconversion. In the beginning, inquisitions were local ecclesial courts of inquiry temporarily called into session as circumstances demanded, though later they became permanent in many places. The chief inquisitor was a cleric, often a bishop, usually with a theological and legal background. He and his assistants were to sniff out heretics, torture them until they admitted their guilt, and then turn them over to the state for execution, right?

So says contemporary opinion, which happens to be all wrong. To understand the truth about the Inquisition it must be first understood that the Church needed to investigate cases of heresy because the salvation of souls was at stake. For a Catholic to renounce the faith and join a heretical sect made him an apostate in danger of losing his soul and going to hell. Moreover, he might lead others to damnation, and in the case of some of the heretical cult leaders, he could become a rebel against the government and bring chaos to the state. The matter, in short, was most serious (in a way that the modern indifferentist mind cannot easily grasp); the inquisitor's main task was not to condemn the heretic but to save his soul. To this end we find inquisitors spending days patiently explaining to heretics where their errors lay and trying to get them to renounce them for their own good. If the inquisitor brought back one of those souls, he had succeeded; if the heretic remained unreconciled, the inquisitor had failed.

One powerful medieval heresy with which the Inquisition had to contend was the Cathar sect, also known as the Albigensian heresy because it came to dominate parts of the region of Albi in southern France. This bizarre movement had features found in ancient Gnostic cults and in Buddhism, though some of its adherents claimed St. Paul as their spiritual ancestor. It spread in a shadowy, secretive fashion throughout the Balkans, into Italy, and surfaced in the 12th century in the western German states before taking root in Albi.

The previous period, from the 10th through the early 11th centuries, had been a low point for the Church in many ways. Attempts by lay authorities to gain control over the bishops and even the popes had to be combated, as did the widespread ignorance and moral corruption of the clergy (and the laity, of course, who produce the clergy) that had begun in the Dark Ages. Many priests still had concubines or "wives" and were otherwise unfit for their offices, and the scandalized laity were vulnerable to sects that claimed to be holier than the Church. Thus the Cathars played on Catholic ignorance and dissatisfaction, contrasting their own supposed purity of life with that of the corrupt priests. (It is noteworthy that they had the most success in a fairly isolated region of France that had probably remained untouched by the great Gregorian Reform of the Church that had begun in the late 11th century.)

By the time we find it in France, Albigensianism had acquired a number of sinister features that brought it into conflict with both the Church and the royal French government. It cannot strictly be called a heresy because there was little of Christianity in it. It was actually a murky dualism, with a god of good and a god of evil; matter was evil and spirit was good, and the goal of life was to rise above the material world. Accordingly, the Cathars frowned on procreation, and when they reached a satisfactory point in their spiritual progress some refused food and drink so that they would die and be *really* free of material things. (Lest they have second thoughts, their brethren would kindly see to it that they went ahead with the plan—if necessary by holding them down in order to keep them from food.) It is obvious that such a creed was antisocial to the core; literally adhered to, it would mean the disappearance of the human race, though its peasant disciples probably did not think that through.

Saints of the time, such as Bernard of Clairvaux, tried to convert the Cathars but with little success. In the 13th century, Pope Innocent III encouraged attempts at conversion by the Dominicans, who served as papal legates to southern France. St. Dominic himself managed to win over (or back) a few, but others among his confreres were murdered before they had a chance to begin their mission. It seems the Cathars had gained the support of local lords who were anxious for independence from the central government; eventually this led to a civil war at the end of which both the political revolt and the Cathar movement were largely suppressed. Catharism did, however, survive in mountain villages, about one of which we have the detailed records of an inquisitor, Bishop Jacques Fournier, the future Avignon Pope Benedict XII.

An Inquisitor at Work

The records provide great insight into how these zealots intruded into every aspect of life—especially in an isolated mountain village such as Montaillou where the local priest was unlikely to be a match for them and the small farmers and shepherds were willing to listen to something new from someone who cultivated an air of authority. Cathar prejudice against women meant that men were generally the targets of the preachers, though there were women adherents of the sect also. In fact the records speak of one woman praying the Hail Mary who was scolded by her companion on the grounds that their Cathar director had told them not to pray to our Lady. The records also contain the account of a mother who had been persuaded to stop nursing her baby so that he could die and be among the Perfect, and how she could not bear to hear him crying with hunger and started feeding him again—to the great disapproval of her Cathar associates.

Bishop Fournier's meticulous records involving Montaillou and the surrounding area comprise 94 cases and hundreds of interrogations. He spent hundreds of days on these cases, patiently asking questions and enduring long, rambling answers. In only one case, which government agents forced him to bring against lepers who were accused of poisoning wells, did he allow torture, according to French historian Le Roy Ladurie, who used Fournier's register to write his book on Montaillou. He does not, however, give any details of this leper case, and other historians of the Inquisition state that Fournier never used torture. This is probable, since the use of torture was adopted into civil law only in the 13th century. Even then, when the Church began to use it in heresy investigations, it was strictly limited by the rules of Inquisitorial courts. It could be used only once, only as a last resort and only to gain necessary information, and it could not last more than a few minutes or be severe enough to cause lasting injury.

But we are in the 14th century now, and our inquisitor is spending all his time listening to heretics, not torturing them. His motivation, writes Ladurie, "was the desire . . . to know the truth. For him, it was a matter first of detecting sinful behavior and then of saving souls."[56] He showed great patience and persistence in trying to bring minds and hearts to the truth; in the case of one Jew, who somehow got mixed up with the crowd being questioned, the bishop spent two weeks explaining to him the doctrine of the Trinity, which the man seems to have then accepted; a week on gaining his assent to the doctrine of Christ's two natures; and three more weeks on the advent of the Messiah.[57]

Fournier's method of patient listening, conversation, and teaching of true doctrine had a positive effect; it seems that all, or nearly all, the villagers were reconciled to the Church—a good

---

[56] Ladurie, p. xv.
[57] Ibid.

example of success in a difficult undertaking of reconversion. Coming up with the exact number of reconversions in medieval heresy cases is impossible; people in those days did not think in statistical terms, though we do find total numbers of cases and so forth recorded by some inquisitors in some of the records that have survived. We have accounts of investigations in earlier medieval centuries that seem almost casual. A Catholic found guilty of professing some heretical doctrine would have it carefully explained to him and be given a penance. This could range from making a pilgrimage, to wearing a distinctive mark on his clothes for a period of time, to imprisonment. Even if put in jail, if he became ill or his family needed him he could be allowed to go home and come back to finish his sentence later. It seems to have been a system that worked.

Undoubtedly, public censure of heresy and those promoting it, on the part of both Church and state, played a large role in Catholic Christendom's lasting as long as it did. Had the one true Church and its teaching not been protected and cultivated as they were, Europe would have seen much sooner the distressing situation produced by the Reformation—with the principle of private judgment leading to Protestantism's fragmentation into numerous sects, even during the lifetimes of the original heresiarchs.

Heresy, Schism, and Subjugation

In the disturbed atmosphere of the late Middle Ages—the 14th century alone saw the Black Death, the Hundred Years' War, and the Great Schism—a number of influential movements surfaced. One was the Flagellants, who after the Black Death could be found traveling from town to town, publicly scourging themselves to appease the justice of the God who had struck the world with plague. The Church had condemned similar movements in the past for their eccentric teachings and rituals, tendencies towards anti-Semitism, or other undesirable elements. But the one that emerged after the Black Death grew to such a large scale—affecting much of Europe—and its unorthodox preaching created so much hysteria and even occasional violence that the Flagellants became the objects of papal censure and suppression by lay authorities. Though some of them may have been good, even saintly people in their penitential motives, as a whole the Flagellants exemplified the numerous heterodox movements of this uneasy period of history, prefiguring the Protestant revolution that was soon to come.

John Wycliffe began another such movement of the 14th century in England (which, interestingly, had never taken to the Flagellants). He started out as a student and then professor at Oxford, where he seems to have absorbed some of the questionable philosophical ideas of William of Occam. He became involved in various controversies over the respective roles of Church and state in England and grew increasingly dissatisfied with the Church; it must, he thought, be thoroughly reformed by the state if necessary. He called for radical clerical poverty, espoused a heretical doctrine of predestination and belief in Scripture as the sole rule of faith, and attacked papal authority and the doctrine of transubstantiation. The Church condemned his heretical ideas after his death (banning his writings and even exhuming and incinerating his corpse), but they survived among his followers, known as the Lollards.

In a fateful development, those ideas made an unlikely migration to Bohemia via the members of the Queen of England's retinue. Queen Anne of Bohemia had come to England a few years after Wycliffe's death and seems to have shown some interest in his work; certainly some of her servants did, and they brought them back home when they returned to Bohemia. There a priest named Jan Hus found them most interesting and incorporated them into what became known as the Hussite heresy—another one of those movements in which doctrinal error and political goals (in this case, more autonomy for Bohemia within the Holy Roman Empire) were mixed. When Hus was executed after the Council of Constance found him guilty of heresy in 1415—a much debated action because Hus had been promised safe conduct there—it was the signal for a series of wars of independence that added not only to the instability of Europe but to the growth of heresy, as Hussite ideas spread throughout the Germanic states and even into Hungary and some of the Balkan states.

The Hussites—who almost immediately, in good Protestant fashion, divided into two religious factions—began agitation against Catholics in 1419: driving priests from their parishes, expelling Catholics from the Bohemian cities the Hussites took over (and sometimes just killing them), and rebuffing attempts at reconciliation with the Church. Since Bohemia was part of the Holy Roman Empire, the emperor became involved, the pope agreed to call a crusade to help suppress the rebels, and neighboring countries and provinces of the empire sent troops. (Even St. Joan of Arc, who had heard about the war and was moved by the atrocities committed by the Hussites against civilians, wrote them a letter threatening them with dire consequences unless they gave up their heresy.[58]) The Hussites paid back those neighbors by sending punitive expeditions to terrorize their people. It was not until 1434 that they were finally suppressed; when the Reformation erupted in the following century, some of the Hussites seem to have become either Lutherans or Calvinists—no doubt among the most combative ones.

Given the chaotic nationalism that was the legacy of Hus, and the bitterness that was exacerbated by military defeat in the Hussite wars, the Church had little chance of winning back the Czechs. This would also be the case elsewhere, when nationalism—and sometimes economic interests—reinforced heresy.

Southeastern Europe also saw the emergence of radical heretical movements in the late medieval period. In the Balkan Peninsula, the shadowy Bogomil sect—reminiscent of dualistic

---

[58] Williamson, Allen. Joan of Arc's Letter to the Hussites (March 23, 1430). March 30, 2010. Joan of Arc Archive. February 29, 2012 <http://archive.joan-of-arc.org/joanofarc_letter_march_23_1430.html>

Catharism—managed to appeal to people with axes to grind (whether religious, political, or economic). Bosnia's Hungarian overlords attempted to suppress it with force, but it proved fairly tenacious. Then there was the so-called "Bosnian Church," a movement begun by a group of monasteries that had somehow gone their own way and begun pulling peasants of the countryside into schism.

Rome and Catholic Hungary made repeated efforts to enlighten the Bosnians by sending missionaries. In the 1430s, the Franciscans began to have considerable success in winning over Bogomils, Bosnian Church members, some Orthodox, many of the nobility, and even pockets of Hussites. The presence of St. Jacob de Marchia, who became the Franciscan vicar in 1435, stimulated the conversion and reconversion efforts and the building of new churches. Some hundreds of thousands seem to have been converted during this decade, but an even greater threat loomed: the Turks, who had been drawing ever closer to mastery of the Balkans, moved into Bosnia in force in the 1460s and crushed the last pockets of resistance in 1482.

Bogomilism and the Bosnian Church disappeared with the Turkish conquest; it is thought that some of the Bosnians who converted to Islam under Turkish rule came from the ranks of discontented Bogomils and schismatics. But other defectors to Islam in Bosnia, Albania (after the defeat of the Catholic resistance hero Skanderbeg), and even Hungary had been at least nominal Catholics, and their reconversion posed a new problem for the Church. The motives of these apostates were mixed; certainly there was economic profit in embracing the conquerors' religion, as the subsequent land distribution in Bosnia—with the landlords Muslim and the intransigent Christians serfs—demonstrates. Muslim converts enjoyed privileges (their sons would not be forcibly taken from them and sent to serve the sultan, for example) while the Christians were left in *dhimmitude*, a state of permanent subservience to their Muslim overlords that could affect everything from the type and color of the clothing they wore to the size of their houses. The Church seems to have had no great success in winning back these former Catholics, perhaps in part because of the notorious death penalty for "apostasy" imposed by the Muslim authorities; despite the eventual expulsion of the Ottoman Turks by the West, nearly half the Bosnian population remains Muslim today.

There were other movements, other currents of dissatisfaction with doctrines or practices of the Church in the 14th and 15th centuries, many calls for reform by both Catholics and heretics, but we will have to leave them and get on to the tragic blowup that was the Reformation. More particularly, we want to see how the Church, particularly during the Counter-Reformation, coped with the formidable task of reconverting the Protestants.

The Problem of
Converting the "Reformed"

The unhappy movement known as the Protestant Reformation began in 1517 with the German priest Martin Luther, who defied Church authority by promulgating such heretical notions as the total depravity of man, salvation by faith alone (*sole fide*) apart from works, and infallible spiritual authority from the Bible alone (*sola scriptura*) apart from the Church. He also charmingly asserted that "reason is the Devil's whore; it must be drowned at baptism." A mixed bag, and rather repellent, one might say, but Luther's notions resounded with the latent anti-Romanism of the Germans, with German princes espousing Lutheranism as a weapon against the Catholic Holy Roman Emperor, and with early nationalists: "I am the prophet of the Germans!" Luther said, as Hus was the prophet of the Bohemians. Everywhere the new religions of the Reformation would be mixed with nationalism.

That was one brand new religion. Meanwhile John Calvin, the French-born preacher of predestination who believed that human nature was even more depraved than Luther thought it was, created a little theocratic state in Geneva where his stern—to say the least—principles were put into practice. His ideas spread into French-speaking areas, and in France, as with Lutheranism in Germany, they became political weapons against the Catholic monarchs.

That's two. There remains, besides all the splinter groups that those new religions spawned—on the principle of private judgment that makes every man his own pope—the land of England. After the Church refused to annul his marriage so that he could wed his mistress, the celebrated lecher and unlikely heresiarch Henry VIII declared himself the head of the Church in England in 1534. There too, the new religion became a useful tool for nationalists and greedy nobles, leading to the seizing and despoiling of Church property and a great persecution of those who adhered to the old religion. This intensified under the long reign of Henry's daughter Elizabeth, making many martyrs and solidifying the establishment of a counterfeit Catholicism in England.

Here, then, was the overwhelming challenge to the Church at the end of the 16th century: Christendom, that large family of the Catholic nations of Europe, had been smashed apart into mutually incompatible pieces, apparently forever. The Church did not surrender without a fight, however, and in the short term it had spectacular success in reconverting some of the apostate lands and keeping others within the fold.

The Catholic Reformation

The rise of the Reformation was like the shock of cold water to a clerical bureaucracy that had become complacent, tolerant of clerical worldliness and moral corruption, and uncritical of popes who lived like the Renaissance princes they were, preoccupied with Italian politics. It was not that there had been no movements aimed at reform; there had been, but getting their ideas implemented was another matter. The bureaucracy of the international Church had grown so large, its inertia so endemic, that a system that had worked fine in the earlier, peaceful centuries simply could not get things done. The impetus for change had to come from the top, and the early 16th-century popes were far below the standard of what was required.

Then in 1534 Paul III came to the papal throne. Though not a shining example of personal morality, he took some steps of great historical significance: In 1540 he recognized the Society of Jesus, then being formed by Ignatius Loyola and his companions, and he called the Council of Trent in 1545. Both these decisions were to have tremendous consequences for the cause of reconversion in a spiritually devastated Christendom. Prior to those two moves, in 1537, he promulgated a bull forbidding the enslavement of the Indians in the Americas, and the following year excommunicated Henry VIII. Pope Paul III also took other measures to fight corruption within the Church, though they did not get very far, and the German Protestants mocked him for his lack of success. His main achievements were not projects that he himself completed but the many good things he put in motion: the Jesuits, the Council of Trent, the freedom of the Indians. After Trent, its decrees concerning the reform of seminaries, the education of monks and priests, clerical morality, and much more were distributed throughout the West, secretly if necessary, as in places where the political authorities were already strongly Protestant.

God's Secret Agents

In the 16th and 17th centuries, Catholic reformers turned up by the hundreds throughout Europe to aid in the reconversion of the West. Their number, achievements, and holiness are almost unprecedented in Christian history. Most prominent were the Jesuits, who would soon be found all over the world, from the Far East to the Americas—where we have already see them—as well as in almost every European country. In the new Protestant countries, where Catholic churches were demolished or turned into heretic temples, monasteries closed and their assets seized, and priests required to submit to the new regime under penalty of exile or death, there was a brief window of opportunity in many places before the heretics gained complete control, and to exploit that window required courage and tact.

Ignatius's instructions to his Jesuits are full of practical advice as well as general exhortations to gentleness, friendliness, and helpfulness. Addressing a group (which included St. Peter Canisius) assigned to positions in the University of Ingolstadt, where heresy was making inroads, he stressed that lectures on doctrine should avoid "many technical terms" and "be learned . . . yet not longwinded."[59] Furthermore, they "should make efforts to make friends with the leaders of their opponents, as also with those who are most influential among the heretics. . . . They must try to bring them back from their error by sensitive skill and signs of love."[60]

Highly intelligent, educated, disciplined, steeped in a vigorous spirituality adapted to their times, the Jesuits did so much to restore the faith in Europe, and to spread it throughout the world, that it would take volumes to tell it all. Where a prince or monarch was uncertain what to do about militant Protestantism in his realm, he would often find himself visited by a diplomat from somewhere, or an elegantly dressed merchant, who turned out to be a Jesuit come to advise him, bringing a message from the pope. They were clever at disguises that enabled them to circulate, like St. Edmund Campion, in enemy territory—comforting the faithful, reconciling heretics, dispensing the sacraments, identifying the errors of Protestantism, and promoting the restoration of the Church as far as they could. Campion did all this in England, before his capture, torture, and horrible martyrdom by hanging, drawing, and quartering. Other Jesuits took his place and many shared his fate.

On the continent, a fine example of a holy and gifted "reconverter" was St. Francis de Sales, who became bishop of Geneva. (Although, since Calvin and his early followers had set up a

---

[59] Lualdi, p. 212.
[60] Ibid., p. 213.

"godly commonwealth" in Geneva, where Catholics—like fancy clothes, dancing, and gambling—were forbidden, the bishop's seat was at nearby Annecy.) He had been born in the Duchy of Savoy, and when a portion of that territory, the Chablais, fell to Calvinism, he volunteered to try to win it back to the faith.

When he began his mission, it was said that the district had 72,000 Calvinists but only 27 Catholics. Tirelessly traveling and preaching throughout the area, he won hearts with his kindness and holiness, and minds with his learning; he debated Calvinist preachers sent out from Geneva and confounded them in argument; he wrote tracts and pamphlets defending the Catholic faith. By the time St. Francis left the region two years later, it was said that the 72,000 Calvinists were now 72,000 Catholics, and there were only 27 Calvinists left. (We hope they were not the 27 who were counted as Catholics before.)

There is much more to his career and his many achievements, but through them all his gentleness, kindness, and ability to discuss matters of faith with both simplicity and clarity come through. Francis de Sales represents the ideal of the Counter-Reformation: to win back erring souls in a way that made them experience the attractiveness, as well as the truth, of the Catholic faith they had once rejected.

Thus were some of the heretics converted, many states kept faithful, and Catholic remnants succored in states where the faith was lost. And indeed the toll was great. England was gone and the Irish severely persecuted as a result. France was partly saved but divided; the Calvinist Huguenots would be granted not only toleration but also the right to their independent cities and armed forces. Spain and Portugal remained faithful, as did the Italian states, more or less. The countries of Scandinavia became wholly Protestant, as did the north German states, where Luther had got his start. Southern German states such as Bavaria, however, remained Catholic, as did Austria and the Holy Roman Emperor as a unit—though it would break up into Protestant and Catholic states in the course of the following centuries.

What of the eastern countries? The Reformation split Hungary too, with Hungarian Calvinists gaining great and enduring influence in certain parts of the country. The Church in Poland, meanwhile, had been in a bad way at the time of the Reformation. The clergy was greatly in need of reform; many priests were leading worldly lives and the faithful's dissatisfaction with them led to the infiltration of Hussite and Calvinist ideas and to talk of a Polish national church. Before permanent damage could be done, some Catholic bishops finally discovered their backbones, and the Jesuits arrived. By the 17th century, Poland was once more a strong Catholic nation.

The Fortress-Shrine

Still, the Jesuits are only partly to thank. There was also the influence of our Lady, seen most dramatically in the defeat of a Swedish army that threatened to make the country Lutheran.

Pilgrims to Poland often visit the high-walled monastery of Jasna Gora and its church where the ancient icon of our Lady is on display, located near the city of Czestochowa. Her picture is not perfect: there is a deep gash across the right side of the face (the Hussites stole it in 1430, then slashed it and threw it to the ground when their horses refused to move) and the image is unusually dark. As with some other venerated images of our Lady of ancient but unknown origin, this "Black Madonna" was said to have been painted by St. Luke. It probably arrived at the monastery from somewhere in the east, after sojourns in various places including Hungary, whence it was presented to the monks at Jasna Gora in the 14th century. Many graces and miracles are associated with the image, perhaps the most spectacular of them the saving of Poland from Lutheran conquest.

In 1655 the new Lutheran king of Sweden decided to take over Poland and very nearly did so. In an invasion known in Polish history as "the Deluge," he captured Warsaw with little trouble, and the Polish king fled while his army dispersed. With much of the country under Swedish control, bringing widespread destruction and plundering, the Swedish army under the German General Müller attempted to take the well fortified monastery at Jasna Gora, probably because there was said to be much treasure there in the form of offerings left by pilgrims over the centuries.

The job proved uncommonly difficult. The gunners manning the fortifications, under the direction of their indomitable prior Augustine Kordecki, were accurate; the local inhabitants burned their own houses to prevent the Swedes from finding cover; there were instances of cannonballs bouncing off the monastery walls instead of exploding. The general himself was said to have seen a lady in shining garments on the walls, tossing back the Swedish shells.

After over a month of siege, the last assault was set for Christmas Day. The Swedes had been receiving reinforcements, mostly German mercenaries, and with at least 3,000 soldiers they now greatly outnumbered the defenders. They first offered to withdraw on payment of a large ransom, but Kordecki replied that although he would have paid it at the beginning of the siege, now he needed the money for repairs. And so the assault began while the monks celebrated the holy day within the fortress; some of the besiegers thought they were celebrating their victory and became confused and demoralized. Two days later, they withdrew. They had lost several hundred men while the Poles, who had saved the last unconquered fortress in the country, lost but a few dozen. The following year, 1656, King John II Casimir proclaimed Our Lady of Częstochowa as Queen and Protector of Poland. Thanks to her, Poland is still Catholic today.[61]

What conclusions can be drawn from this overview of reconversion in the medieval and early modern eras? There would

---

[61] The courageous Prior Kordecki, certainly a priest with a sense of humor, wrote a detailed account of the siege, of which only some details are given here. His story is well worth reading online.

seem to be at least three main factors that tended to erode faith and produce apathy or hostility among Catholics in those centuries and thus make them vulnerable to heretical teaching. The first was widespread ignorance and immorality among the clergy, including a few notoriously immoral popes, which scandalized the faithful and left them prey to heretics and sects. Secondly, the development of nationalism in the early modern world was a potent force that favored heretics such as Luther and Hus, who played the role of national prophets; England was similarly influenced by clever Protestant nationalist propaganda during the reign of Elizabeth. Such propaganda played on the "foreign" character of Catholicism, with the pope far away in Rome, wallowing in immorality and luxury and draining the nation's resources by collecting the hated tithes. Lastly, the influence of temporal rulers in religious affairs increased throughout the period. Their example had always been important, as we have seen in numerous cases of early barbarian conversions, but it became far more critical during the Reformation when the ruler of England made himself the head of the English church and Luther gave German princes control over religious affairs. This is why Catholic missionaries were so anxious to win back monarchs who had apostatized or, failing that, to reconvert whoever would succeed them.

To counter these three influences, the Council of Trent (convened in 1545) instituted wide-ranging reforms. The establishment of seminaries throughout Christendom, not just Europe, helped reduce clerical ignorance. Clerical immorality was severely dealt with at all levels, and it is heartening to note that the pope who zealously implemented the Tridentine reforms near the end of the 16th century—Pope St. Pius V—was also a saint. Since religious nationalism was partially fueled by the lack of native priests and by absentee bishops who collected heavy tithes but spent most of their time outside their dioceses, the new local seminaries and the Council's requirement that bishops live in their sees—as well as being sufficiently educated and virtuous—helped defuse the appeal of purely national churches. Rulers in Catholic countries were encouraged to be examples to their people and to promote their religious education and welfare, and advisors—often Jesuits—were sent to counsel them as the need arose. Many a timid ruler facing a growing tide of Protestantism within his country found his backbone stiffened by prudent advice from informed clergy.

These provisions were all good, but of course the critical element was the personnel who implemented them. If the same mediocre, ignorant, or immoral clerics who had scandalized so many Catholics were charged with carrying out the Council's provisions, the status quo would not change, no matter how many seminaries were established. In one of those tremendous divine surprises that punctuate history, the reformers God raised up to restore and revitalize Christendom in the period following the Council of Trent were not only numerous but also, one might almost say disproportionately, saints. The founders of the new and dynamic religious orders that would do so much to transform the world were saints: Ignatius and his many canonized Jesuits; Teresa of Avila and John of the Cross with their Carmelite Reform; Francis de Sales and Jane de Chantal and the Visitation Order; Philip Neri and his Oratory, making Rome again a holy city; Vincent de Paul creating the first organized charitable network for relief of the poor—these are only some of the postconciliar reformers who changed the face of Catholicism following the Protestant Revolt. They were bishops, priests, popular preachers, missionaries, teachers of children, diplomats, and lay men and women, and they accomplished wonders. Slowly the missionaries of reconversion not only repaired and preserved what remained of Christendom but, like Francis de Sales in the Chablais, they won back countless souls.

ℬ INSTRUMENTS OF CONVERSION ℰ

THE PRINTED WORD

The mechanical object known as the printing press might not seem at first glance to be an instrument of conversion, and in fact it was widely used by heretics to disseminate their false doctrines not long after its invention in the 15th century. Once the saints of the Counter-Reformation began to make use of it, however, it proved to have a great power for good.

To correct the erroneous editions of Scripture used by the Protestants, Catholic Bibles were printed and disseminated. Printed documents helped spread knowledge of papal condemnations of heresies, and printed catechisms combated ignorance of Church teaching among Catholics. Catechetical translations into various languages—including those spoken by the various Indian tribes of Spanish America—proved invaluable tools for missionaries. Since not everyone could afford a book, apologists and missionaries made use of printed pamphlets and tracts, as St. Francis de Sales did in his spiritual war with the Calvinists. The printed word, whether found in paper books, booklets, and tracts, or "printed" virtually in electronic documents, remains a powerful instrument of conversion in our media age.

The Work of Conversion Goes On

The souls of our age may be the most difficult in history to evangelize. The Roman pagans were willing to be convinced by the truth when it was presented to them. The Arians gradually gave up their heresy, as did the disciples of the Cathars. Even Calvinists were converted when St. Francis de Sales explained Catholic teaching clearly to them. Those peoples accepted the existence of religious truth; they were willing to listen with relatively open minds; they could follow an argument and they cared deeply about knowing the truth.

Today it is hard to find people with any of these basic qualities. Moral and intellectual relativism dominate our Western culture. Sexual immorality is rampant on a scale that would have scandalized a pagan Roman. Secularist assumptions inform all our public institutions. Ubiquitous media distractions have robbed this generation of the ability to think clearly, follow arguments, and concentrate for long periods.

There is no historical parallel that I can see for such formidable obstacles to belief coming together at the same time. There are, however, two historical developments that provide reason to hope that even our age might be converted.

The first was the great progress in all areas of Catholic conversion and reform produced by the Council of Trent, so important that it is given a special section in history textbooks under the name Counter-Reformation. The great reform it called for would have remained a dead letter were it not for the extraordinary crop of saints that God raised up to carry it out. We can hope that a new dogmatic council (Vatican III?) will be called to confront the grave problems the Church now faces, and that God will again bring forth saintly preachers, theologians, educators, missionaries, and reformers of religious orders to dent the apathy and disbelief of our age.

The second historical event was the stunning conversion of the peoples of the former Aztec Empire, at a time when it seemed that their alienation from their conquerors was growing. God, so to speak, gave the Spaniards 10 years, from the conquest of 1521 to 1531, and when they failed to give him the souls he wanted, he sent his Mother to do the job. We saw how spectacularly she accomplished it, with millions of the Mexicans entering the Church soon after her appearance. Similarly, in a year of overwhelming and tragic historical importance, she appeared at Fatima with a number of messages for the little shepherds she visited to pass on to Church authorities. World War I would soon end, she said, but if men did not stop offending God another one, even worse, would come. Our Lady therefore asked for Communions of Reparation on the first Saturdays, penance, and certain prayers, including the rosary, with an extra prayer to be said after each decade. She made other requests of the hierarchy, but prayer, penance, devotion to her Immaculate Heart and to the rosary in particular were practices that all Catholics were urged to adopt. Just as she gave victory to the Christian fleet over the Turks at the Battle of Lepanto, when Christendom followed the pope in praying the rosary fervently for that intention, and gave the Church in Mexico millions of converts by her intercession, so she can perform miracles of conversion (and reconversion) today if only she is asked with the Marian prayers and devotions that have been given to the Church in our time. We are, after all, privileged to live in the Age of Mary, which began in the 19th century with a series of extraordinary apparitions that demonstrated our Lady's concern for the Church in the modern world. From the Rue de Bac to La Salette, Lourdes, Fatima, and elsewhere, her messages give evidence of the love of God for mankind by his sending of his Mother, the Mediatrix of all the graces we stand so much in need of—the graces of conversion and reconversion among them.

We must not end on a note of doom, then; we are bid to "rejoice always," and doing God's will in all circumstances, as well as practicing the devotions for which heaven specifically asked, cannot only bring us joy and peace but promote the coming of the kingdom of God in the world. That coming may seem stalled just now, but we know by faith that it is even now proceeding with the conversion or reconversion of souls, one by one by one.

Bibliography

Arendzen, John, "Manichæism," *The Catholic Encyclopedia.* Vol. 9. (New York: Robert Appleton Company, 1910).

Ashe, Geoffrey, *The Discovery of King Arthur* (London: Guild Publishing, 1985).

Bakay, Kornél, "Hungary," Chapter 21, *The New Cambridge Medieval History*, vol. III (Cambridge University Press, [2005] 2006).

Barry, Colman J., O.S.B., ed., *Readings in Church History* (Westminster, Md.: Christian Classics, Inc., 1985).

Bede, Saint (The Venerable), *A History of the English Church and People* (Harmondsworth, England: Penguin Books, [1955] 1972).

Caraman, Philip S.J., *The Lost Paradise: The Jesuit Republic in South America* (New York: Dorset Press, 1975).

Carroll, Warren E., *Our Lady of Guadalupe and the Conquest of Darkness* (Front Royal, Va.: Christendom Press, 1993).

_____, *The Building of Christendom* (Front Royal, Va.: Christendom Press, 1987).

_____, *The Cleaving of Christendom* (Front Royal, Va.: Christendom Press, 2000).

Daniel-Rops, Henri, *The Church of the Apostles and Martyrs* (New York: E.P. Dutton & Company Inc., [1948] 1963).

_____, *The Church in the Dark Ages* (New York: E.P. Dutton & Company Inc., [1959] 1969).

D'arras, M. l'Abbé J.E., *A General History of the Catholic Church* (New York: P. O'Shea Publisher, 1866).

Dienes, István, *The Hungarians Cross the Carpathians* (Budapest: Corvina Press, 1972).

Duckett, Eleanor Shipley, *Anglo-Saxon Saints and Scholars* (New York: The Macmillan Company, 1947).

_____, *Carolingian Portraits: A Study in the Ninth Century* (Ann Arbor, Mich.: University of Michigan Press, [1962] 1969).

_____, *Death and Life in the Tenth Century* (Ann Arbor, Mich.: University of Michigan Press, [1967] 1968).

_____, *Alfred the Great: The King and His England* (Chicago: University of Chicago Press, [1956] 1965).

_____, *The Gateway to the Middle Ages: France and Britain* (Ann Arbor, Mich.: University of Michigan Press, [1938] 1964).

Dukes, Eugene D., *Magic and Witchcraft in the Dark Ages* (Lanhom, New York: University Press of America, [1972] 1996).

Egyed, Hermann, *A katolikus egyháztörténete Magyarországon 1914-ig* (Munich: Aurora Könyvek, 1973).

Fine, John V.A. Jr., *The Late Medieval Balkans* (Ann Arbor, Mich.: University of Michigan Press, [1994] 1996).

Fletcher, Richard, *The Barbarian Conversion* (New York: Henry Holt and Company, [1997] 1998).

Fliche, Augustin and Martin, Victor, eds., *Histoire de l'Eglise*, vols. 2, 3, 4 (Paris: Bloud & Gay, 1943, 1947, 1948).

Fox, Robin Lane, *Pagans and Christians* (New York: Alfred A. Knopf, [1986] 1987).

Ghéon, Henri, *St. Martin of Tours* (New York: Sheed and Ward, 1946).

Grant, Michael, *Constantine the Great* (New York: Charles Scribner's Sons, [1993] 1994).

Halecki, Oscar, *The Borderlands of Western Civilization* (New York: Ronald Press Company, 1952).

Hanke, Lewis, *The Spanish Struggle for Justice in the Conquest of America* (Boston, Massachusetts: Little, Brown and Company, 1965).

Kamen, Henry, *The Spanish Inquisition: A Historical Revision* (London: The Folio Society, [1965] 1998).

Ker, W.P., *The Dark Ages* (New York: New American Library of World Literature, 1958).

Keyes, Frances Parkinson, *St. Anne, Grandmother of Our Saviour* (New York: Julian Messner, 1955).

Krmpotic, Martin Davorin, "Croatia," *Catholic Encyclopedia*, vol. 4.(New York: Robert Appleton Company, 1908).

Ladurie, Le Roy, *Montaillou: The Promised Land of Error* (New York: George Braziller, Inc., [1975] 1978).

László, Gyula, *The Magyars: Their Life and Civilization* (Budapest: Corvina Books, 1996).

Lot, Ferdinand, *The End of the Ancient World and the Beginning of the Middle Ages* (New York: Harper and Row, [1931] 1965).

Luardi, Katharine J. ed., *Sources of the Making of the West: A Concise History*, vol. 1, 2nd edition (Boston: Beford; New York: St. Martin's, 2007).

MacManus, Seumas, *The Story of the Irish Race* (New York: Devin-Adair Company, [1944] 1967).

Marrou, H.I., *A History of Education in Antiquity* (Sheed and Ward, 1956).

McCartney, C.A., *Hungary: A Short History* (Edinburgh: University Press, 1962).

Moczar, Diane, *Islam at the Gates* (Manchester, N.H.: Sophia Institute Press, 2008).

Mondot, Jean-François, "Geneviève, une sainte engagée," in "Paris raconte Lutèce," (*Les Cahiers de Science et Vie*, no. 111, June-July 2009).

Moran, Patrick Francis Cardinal, "St. Palladius," *Catholic Encyclopedia*, vol. 11. (New York: Robert Appleton Company, 1911).

Mindszenty, Joseph Cardinal, *The World's Most Orphaned Nation* (New York: Julius Tarlo, 1962).

Mourret, Fernand, *Les Peres de l'Eglise,* vol. 2 of *Histoire Generale de l'Eglise* (Paris: Bloud & Gay, 1920) and *L' Eglise et le Monde Barbare,* vol. 3, 1921.

Newman, John Henry Cardinal, *The Arians of the Fourth Century* (London/New York: Longmans, Green, and Co., [1833, 1871] 1891).

Perry, Marvin, et al. (eds.), *Sources of the Western Tradition,* vol. 1, 3rd ed. (Boston: Houghton Mifflin Company, 1995).

Pohle. Joseph, "Pelagius and Pelagianism," *Catholic Encyclopedia,* vol. 11. (New York: Robert Appleton Company, 1911).

Powell, Philip Wayne, *Tree of Hate* (New York/London: Basic Books, 1971).

Rand, E. R., *Founders of the Middle Ages* (New York: Dover Publications, [1928] 1957).

Ricciotti, Abbot Guiseppe *Julian the Apostate* (Milwaukee: Bruce Publishing Company, 1960).

Richmond, I.A., *Roman Britain* (Hammondsworth, Middlesex: Penguin Books, 1955).

Rousseau, Paul, *Echternach: Cité abbatiale* (Luxembourg: Editions Guy Binsfeld, undated).

Stancliffe, Clair, "Christianity amongst the Britons, Dalridian Irish and Picts," *New Cambridge Medieval History,* vol. I (Cambridge University Press, [2005] 2006).

Stevenson, Rev. Joseph, ed. and trans., *The Church Historians of England,* vol. II, part II (London: Seeleys, 1854).

Sugar, Peter F., et al., *A History of Hungary* (Bloomington/Indianapolis: Indiana University Press, [1990] 1994).

Szántó, Konrád, O.F.M., *A Katolikus Egyház Története,* vol. I (Budapest: Ecclesia, 1983).

Tóth, Endre, "On the Sources of Pannonian Christianity in the 4th-8th Century and on the Source Value of the Findings," in *Magyar Egyháztörténeti Vázlatok,* vol. 2 (Budapest: Magyar Egyháztörténeti Enciklopédia Munkaközössége, 1991).

Thacker, Alan, "England in the Seventh Century," *New Cambridge Medieval History,* vol. I (Cambridge University Press, [2005] 2006).

Trevor-Roper, Hugh, *The Rise of Christian Europe* (London: Thames and Hudson, 1965, reprint Harcourt, Brace & World, 1970).

Whitelock, Dorothy, *The Beginnings of English Society* (Hammondsworth, Middlesex: Penguin Books, 1952).

Windschuttle, Keith, *The Killing of History* (San Francisco: Encounter Books, 1996).